BESIDE STILL WATERS

Finding Rest in Christ in
Every Season of Motherhood

THE DAILY GRACE CO.®

Contributors

Katie Davidson, Tiffany Dickerson, Krystal Dickson,
Jackie Foster, Gloria Furman, Jennie Heideman, Helen
Hummel, Anne Imboden, Kristyn Perez, Kristin Schmucker,
Anna Elizabeth Taylor, Shelby Turner, Jill Rohrbaugh,
Colleen Wachob, Beth White, and Cassie Whitman

Editors

Helen Hummel, Alli McDougal,
Abby Nieten, and Kristin Schmucker

Table of Contents

WALKING WITH JESUS IN MOTHERHOOD

*Motherhood reminds us that
we are dependent on Jesus
for every moment of our lives.*

Foreword

KRISTIN SCHMUCKER

"Come to me, all who labor and are heavy laden, and I will give you rest."

I read these beautiful words of Jesus in Matthew 11:28 (ESV) and wondered if He had moms in mind. In the beauty of these words is an invitation to anyone, including moms, who labor and are heavy laden. In the long days of motherhood, there have been many times when I have needed rest — rest from my worry; rest from the seemingly endless demands; rest from the expectations that the culture has placed on moms; and rest from, well, just actual rest during the years when a good night's sleep was a distant memory. These words of Jesus remind me that rest is not something I find on my own or that I earn by being good enough — rest is given by Jesus alone.

Motherhood, in all of its beauty and all of its joy, is a reminder to us of our need for Jesus and the rest that only He provides. And though we tend to not like admitting our dependence, motherhood reminds us that we are dependent on Jesus for every moment of our lives. We cannot do this without Him. As the children in our care depend on us, we remember how much we depend on our heavenly Father.

Motherhood is the dream of many little girls, and I was certainly one of them. I dreamt from a young age of rocking babies and buying tiny baby clothes. As I reflect on my one motherhood journey, I can say that motherhood has been far sweeter than I ever could have imagined, and yet it has also brought some of the most heart-wrenching moments of my life. From the tendency of moms to wrap our identity in motherhood to the anxiety we feel over our children's future, motherhood is not always easy. Motherhood is a beautiful dance of joy and uncertainty. Motherhood has brought moments when I have laughed until my side hurt from the funny things my kids have said. It has brought many moments in which I have stood looking at a sleeping child, with my heart about to burst, trying to comprehend how I could love them this much. But, it has also brought moments when I have been gripped with fear and worry over making a wrong decision or not getting this motherhood thing right. It has brought moments when I have basked in the joy of Christmas morning, and it has brought the grief of tragedy and of watching my child face bullying.

As moms, we often feel like our work is unseen and wonder if there is anyone who recognizes the hard work and sleepless nights that we endure for the love of our children. As you read this book, we want you to know that your sisters in Christ here at The Daily Grace Co.® see you, and we want to encourage you on this journey. But more than anything, we want you to know that you are seen by the Lover of your soul. *Jesus sees you*, and He will meet you in this season.

Over the years, our team at The Daily Grace Co. ® has published countless essays—on our blog, in our magazines, and in many other resources—meant to encourage moms in any season of the motherhood journey. Now, for the first time ever, we have compiled some of our favorites of these essays into one place: the book you hold in your hands. It is our hope that these words from moms at every stage will inspire you on your own journey of motherhood and point you to Christ each step of the way.

This book is for the brand new mom who is sleep-deprived and running on empty.

This book is for the mom who has forgotten who she is in the throes of motherhood's demands.

This book is for the mom who wants to be a good mom.

This book is for the mom who wants to glorify God in her motherhood.

This book is for the mom who needs Jesus in her motherhood.

This book is for every mom.

This book is for you.

Identity
in Motherhood

Freedom from Perfection

KRISTYN PEREZ

Should you bottle feed or breastfeed?
Should you homeschool or send your child to public school?
Can your child have Goldfish® or red food dye?

Even though Scripture is silent about a lot questions like these, many moms are not. In fact, there can be a great deal of judgment in motherhood—not only from other moms but also from ourselves. We feel the constant pressure to "do it right," a tension that is only compounded by the quiet judgment of other moms who are looking to feel validated in their decisions and affirmed that they're crushing their role as moms.

Undoubtedly, whether it's your first child or your sixth, you want to be a good mom. You don't want to make unhealthy decisions for your child, so you may wonder, *Are Goldfish® the modern equivalent of bad mothering?* You want to make the best decisions for your children, so you consider, *Is homeschooling the only way to go?* Each second, you wonder, *Am I doing enough? Am I messing up my child? Am I doing a good job? Am I not doing enough?*

Thankfully, there is freedom in Christ to make all kinds of different decisions. God tenderly walks with us in motherhood and equips us with all that we need. He has given us great freedom to make all kinds of parenting decisions, and He has given us the local church to help us grow in our mothering.

OUR FREEDOM IN CHRIST

For freedom, Christ set us free. —Galatians 5:1

As much as we wish it did, Scripture doesn't provide us with many specific answers to our parenting questions, such as:

- What age should I start solids?
- What should I do if my baby has colic?
- How many after-school activities are "too much"?

This can sometimes leave us feeling helpless and alone. But although Scripture doesn't tell us whether to put our children in piano or taekwondo, God does give us everything we need for life and godliness through His Word. He hasn't left us alone to figure out how to be a parent. Instead, He has given us the principles we need to know for parenting in the Bible, as well as the grace to do so each day. He offers us freedom to try new things, to mess up, and to make different decisions—without the overwhelming expectation that we do all things perfectly the first time. He lavishes His grace on us, a gift that offers liberty and strength in the day-to-day moments of mothering. Now, instead of seeking perfection, we can seek the Lord, knowing that He is with us, and He guides each step.

As Galatians 5:1 says, it is for freedom that Christ has set us free. From figuring out how to swaddle our baby to handling the exhaustion of school pick-up, God never abandons or condemns us—not for a second. If we are in Christ, God has given us His Spirit to dwell within us—to guide, convict, help, and remind us of His grace. He knows our weakness, and He does not stand in judgment over us. Instead, He walks with us and helps us to love and parent our children. We never walk alone.

THE SILLINESS OF COMPARISON

Sometimes, though, we can stifle the freedom we have in Christ because we get stuck in the comparison game. We look to the moms around us to determine whether or not we're doing a good job. But God doesn't rank our motherhood successes compared to the mom next door, secretly judging us when our children's shoes are on backwards or when we have spit up on our shirts. He shows grace and showers us with mercy, forgiveness, and freedom!

When we slow down to think about it, it's really silly to compare our lives to our neighbor's, isn't it? After all, our children are completely different. Our lives are completely different. Our financial, emotional, and physical limitations are different. *We* are completely different. We don't need to compete with other moms or worry that we're not doing a good enough job, for God is our help. He loves us and guides us. His grace is sufficient for us.

As we compare ourselves to other moms and try to keep up with the mom next door, we must also remember—we only know a sliver about that mom's life. We know, perhaps, where they went to school and how old their children are, but we don't know the strengths and weaknesses of their childhoods, their deepest fears, and their biggest stressors. We don't know the time they yelled at their children before family photos or bribed them to get to church. With quite limited information, we compare our worst moments with their best ones.

We don't know all the details of another person's life, but God does. He knows not only everything about the mom next door but everything about you. He knows your strengths and weaknesses. He knows what you're good at and what you're not. He knows your fears and your joys. He knows how much certain noises your child makes drive you crazy, and He knows how tired you are of making peanut butter and jelly sandwiches. He knows that there is a part of this specific stage of your parenting that is completely new to you, and He doesn't look down on you, condemning you for all your mistakes. Instead, He offers you His grace and helps you along the way. We don't need to compare ourselves to the mom next door, for we've been offered the sufficiency of Christ.

THE LOCAL CHURCH

At the same time, as you're facing the billion decisions that accompany motherhood, you may be looking for practical help! Even if God doesn't judge you for your family dinner decisions, you'd love help to figure out which options may be best for your family. Thankfully, God has placed us in local families through the local church to help us live out the days God has called us to.

Within the local church, there will be moms who are gifted in ways that we're not, just as we are gifted in ways that others are not. We can look to other moms, not as competitors but as sisters, and ask for guidance along the way. For example, if you see a mom who is wonderful at teaching her children to read and you're about to start that journey with your child, ask for her help! Bring her a coffee one afternoon and ask for advice in teaching children to read. Or if you're months into potty training, instead of feeling like a failure when you hear that one mom potty-trained her child in a weekend, ask her about it! Maybe her child was simply more ready to potty train, or maybe she has wisdom she can share in your potty-training journey. When we stop viewing our child's milestones as a source of pride and when we stop viewing sisters as competition, we can more freely and joyfully ask for help along the way.

God has given us a great gift in the local church as we can encourage one another, not just in Bible reading and prayer but also in everyday faithfulness to our families. He has showered us with His grace and offered us His freedom—freedom from the need to place our identity in our motherhood and to joyfully root it in Christ. His grace sustains us every step of the way.

God tenderly walks with us in motherhood
and equips us with all that we need.

The Old Has Gone, the New Has Come: Gospel Identity in Motherhood

KRYSTAL DICKSON

Motherhood can feel chaotic and uneventful, overwhelming and mundane, all at the same time. We may love the role of mothering while simultaneously struggling to fully embrace all that motherhood entails. If we are not careful, we may resort to "treadmill motherhood," continually taking steps but remaining in place without a destination in sight. Day in and day out, we can go through the motions in an effort to contain the chaos and maintain our sanity. But at the end of the day, what is it all for?

Without a clear vision for our motherhood, we can lose sight of God's desire for us to joyfully embrace our identity in Christ as we disciple our children. We must reorient our focus and widen our perspective to account for more than just the temporary pleasures and challenges of motherhood. In order to do this, we must remember who we are as believers.

Consider what Scripture has to say about who we are: "Therefore, if anyone is in Christ, he is a new creation; the old has passed away, and see, the new has come!" (2 Corinthians 5:17). Though we feel the effects of aging with each passing day, we have been made new, given new life in Christ. This places a calling on us as mothers — to die to ourselves as we bring glory to God.

However, this calling is not unique to motherhood. It is the call we all have as believers. Remembering your calling as a new creation in Christ will rightly orient your heart as you prioritize your identity in Christ before your identity as a mother. The gospel radically transforms how we see ourselves as mothers, casting our roles and responsibilities in a new light. We are so often tempted to define our role as mothers by what we can accomplish—we feed, clothe, teach, chauffeur, clean...the list goes on and on. If we cannot do those things, we feel like we have failed. Yet, in the gospel, we are defined by what Christ accomplished on our behalf.

Jesus did what we never could. His perfect life was laid down as a substitutionary sacrifice for us. By it, we have been made new. We have been reconciled to the Father. We are now the children of God. We are disciples of Jesus Christ. And we are mothers who desire to make (little) disciples who reflect not our glory but the glory of God. We become ambassadors for Christ, ministering to our children as we desire to seek their ultimate good, which is their reconciliation to God (2 Corinthians 5:18–21).

We push back the darkness of this world, living out our identity in Christ as we fulfill our roles in motherhood. With every nose we wipe and every meal we make, we can proclaim the victory of Christ in our lives. Our sacrifices as mothers are not in vain—He sees it all. And not only do we live as new creations here on earth, but we eagerly await the day when Christ returns and makes all things new.

By the goodness of God, we get to see glimpses of His redemptive work even today. As we see men, women, and children come to saving faith in Christ, we are a witness to gospel transformation. The old has gone, and the new has come! The gospel provides a better way for us to live as mothers. It whispers to our weary hearts, "Here, you can rest."

Motherhood is a lifelong endeavor of sacrifice and discipleship that pushes us deeper into our Father's embrace. When we remember that we are new creations in Christ and we have been entrusted with our children, we can rejoice in His kindness and endure difficulties with hope. We do not put value on our days based on how obedient our children are or how productive we are. Instead, we treasure the eternal significance of our ministry in the home. As we continually remind ourselves of the truth and beauty of the gospel, we can disciple our children out of the abundant overflow of grace lavished on us in Christ.

This essay was originally published in issue 3 of Gospel at Home™ *magazine.*

*We can disciple our children out
of the abundant overflow of grace
lavished on us in Christ.*

Mama, Your Work Is Meaningful

KRISTYN PEREZ

Last week, my daughter held a funeral for her pet lizard. She caught the baby lizard just the day before and affectionately named her "Liz." Upon Liz's passing, fresh flowers were picked, and special liturgy music was chosen. The name plaque on Liz's casket had exactly three misspelled words, and every syllable was carefully written with love. The week before, I stood amazed as my two-year-old son said his longest paragraph yet: "Hey sister! That's mine. Give that back to me NOW!" Motherhood sure is a wild ride.

As moms, we are there for the highs and the lows of parenting. We're there for the moments of indescribable love when our hearts feel like they're physically expanding out of affection for our children. We're there for the baby giggles, first words, and "I wuv u's." We're there for the fears shared in the middle of the night and confidences entrusted over cookies and hot chocolate. We're there for the vacations, graduations, and swim meets, and we're eyewitnesses to the subtle (but miraculous!) growth in our children's characters after years of instruction. We are privy to the secret moments of our children's days.

But as moms, we are also there for the harder moments of parenting. We're there for the rebellion and the attitudes. We're there for the broken hearts and skinned knees. We're there for the unnoticed, mundane, around-the-clock tasks. Our days are filled with tantrums from both toddlers and tweens. Our nights are interrupted by baby cries and bad dreams. And at times, we may naturally want to escape the difficult moments of mothering for something greater, something grander.

We want to check off more items from our "to-do" lists. We want rest. We want quiet. We want to go to the bathroom in peace. We want to be able to focus, even if only for a moment.

While none of these desires is inherently wrong, for a season, God has given us the divine privilege of being called "Mom." For a season, quiet may seem to evade us, as peaceful nights spent cozying up with a good book are replaced with nursing babies or teenage troubles. So is it all meaningless? Are we living up to our potential as women if we slow down our busy lives for the little moments—for the lizard funerals, friendship drama, or nighttime snuggles?

As Christians, we know that there is no ordinary moment. Every moment matters when we are living for God's glory, and in every action, we have the opportunity to make much of God (1 Corinthians 10:31). As we are invited into our children's deepest dreams and most tender moments, we have the privilege of being the hands and feet of Jesus to our kids. After all, we follow a Savior who "emptied himself by assuming the form of a servant, taking on the likeness of humanity. And when he had come as a man, he humbled himself by becoming obedient to the point of death—even to death on a cross" (Philippians 2:7–8). Though He was God, Jesus humbled Himself and washed the feet of His friends (John 13:1–17). He let Himself be inconvenienced and spent time with the weak and hurting (Matthew 14:13–21, Mark 3:1–6, Mark 5:21–43). He went without many of life's normal comforts for the sake of loving those around Him (Matthew 8:20). He laid down His life so that we could live (John 3:16).

In the same way, as moms, we have the incredible opportunity to lay our lives down for our children, just like Jesus did for us. We have the blessing of washing dirty toes and comforting hurting hearts. We have the privilege of humbling ourselves in the minute, inconvenient moments of the day. Not only this, but as moms, we have the privilege of knowing our children better than anyone else on the planet. We know when our children are getting sick and when they're overwhelmed. We know what foods they detest and which ones they won't try, even with every form of bribery. Just as God knows us intimately, we are allowed to know and love our children, modeling the love of the Father for them.

We live in a world that tells us to do more and be more. Culture tells us that if we're not in the workplace, we're not living up to our potential. Or, if we are in the workplace, it tells us that we're neglecting our children. Whether or not we work outside the home, when we compare how much we could have gotten done in the day to if we didn't have children, the lists simply do not compare. Yet the life of a Christian is not measured by to-do lists, social climbing, or career advancement. It is not measured by comparing ourselves to the woman next door or by the number of hours we slept. It is measured by grace through faith in God, who is the perfect, all-sufficient, and all-loving parent.

God bids us to make much of Christ in all things, even in mothering. While your daily acts of motherhood may be done in secret, God sees them all. He is pleased when you are loving in the difficult moments, serving when you're tired, and patiently disciplining when it's hard. These small, seemingly unnoticed moments are treasures that are refining you in Christlikeness.

So, mama, your work is meaningful. When you're answering five million "why" questions a day, it matters. When you're handling a teenager's angst with grace, it matters. When you're cooking meals and cleaning up messes, when you're wondering if anyone cares, it matters. When you love your children, you are modeling your Creator by taking the nature of a servant. God sees the hidden moments of your day, and He rejoices in the ways you love your children. Your mothering matters, and when it is done out of love for Christ, it is of infinite worth.

We have the privilege of
being the hands and feet of Jesus to our kids.

This essay was originally published in issue 1 of Gospel at Home™ *magazine.*

God Gives the Growth:
The Tension Between Working
Heartily and Trusting God

KATIE DAVIDSON

Farming, quite frankly, is something I know nothing about. I am about as suburban as they come—a neighborhood kid raised in a midsized home with a midsized dog. Perhaps that's why I was so mesmerized by the cornfields that lined my grandparents' street—how the fields turned from green to golden as the harvest approached; how the sunsets somehow made the fields shine if you were present at just the right time; how the farmers had to trust that the rain, the soil, and the seeds would work together to produce an ample crop.

Now that I'm grown up, I am still mesmerized. In a culture of "want it, get it, have it," these corn fields that still line my grandparents' street seem like a gateway to centuries past—a time when life moved more slowly and dependence upon the Lord was built into daily routines. Though I am sure new technology has emerged, the core tenets of farming remain the same—working, waiting, hoping—sewn together in trust and anticipation of a future harvest.

When I first laid awestruck eyes on my newborn son, I realized that motherhood—quite frankly—was also something I knew nothing about. I had read books, listened to podcasts, and observed my own mom for years, but nothing compared to cradling a swaddled human with a future and potential in my arms—a human who was mine to care for. As much as there was joy, there was also the feeling of, *I hope I don't mess him up.*

As thousands of seeds burrow themselves in soil to create crops, a million decisions add up to make a childhood. Breastfeed or formula feed?

Allow screen time or go screen-free? Public school, private school, or home school? Social media or no social media? Am I being too overprotective? Or not present enough? The options are endless, and so are the questions. The good desire to steward your kids well makes decisions feel weighty—as if you could ruin their future with one bad choice. The weight falls heavily on your shoulders as a mom, doesn't it?

But what if I told you this weight isn't yours to bear on your own?

What if I told you our children's spiritual growth isn't up to us?

GOD GIVES THE GROWTH

In 1 Corinthians 3, the Apostle Paul addresses a tension within the Corinthian church. The church is divided based on their leadership preferences—some want to follow Paul, others a man named Apollos. They are elevating these teachers to celebrity status. In response to this, Paul says:

> *I planted, Apollos watered, but God gave the growth. So, then, neither the one who plants nor the one who waters is anything, but only God who gives the growth. Now he who plants and he who waters are one, and each will receive his own reward according to his own labor. For we are God's coworkers. You are God's field, God's building. (1 Corinthians 3:6–9)*

The Corinthians have placed far too much emphasis on the one who plants and the one who waters while placing far too little emphasis on the One who causes growth in the first place. Planting and watering, on their own, cannot guarantee life. It's not that the teachers' jobs are unimportant—they're essential—but their work is entirely dependent upon God's will to grow.

So, too, we can overemphasize our role in our children's salvation. We can overemphasize our control over our children's lives. Failures feel catastrophic—as if we alone are responsible for our children's lack of faith. Wins feel monumental—we get overly confident in our own abilities. It's not that our jobs as mothers are unimportant. They're essential! God invites us to be examples of His love in our families. God may even use our words—our lessons—to bring our kids to salvation. But we are merely the ones who plant and water—God causes the growth.

What does this mean for us as moms?

ENTRUSTING THE HARVEST TO GOD

We can rest, trusting that the salvation of our children is in God's capable, loving hands. As a farmer works diligently to tend to his crops, we work diligently to teach our kids the truths of Scripture, knowing our labor is not in vain. As a farmer waits expectantly for the rain, we wait expectantly for God to reveal Himself to our children. As a farmer hopes for a bountiful harvest, we hope in prayerful trust that God will save the hearts of our little ones. As a farmer harvests the fruits of his labor, we look expectantly for God's work in our family, praising Him for every bit of fruit we see along the way. We trust in the faithful character of the One who provides growth—for He brought to life what was dead. He died so that we may live.

Consider Paul's reminder to the Ephesian church later in his ministry: "But God, who is rich in mercy, because of his great love that he had for us, made us alive with Christ even though we were dead in trespasses. You are saved by grace!" (Ephesians 2:4–5). In his letter to the Christians in Rome, Paul also explains how God proves His own love to us: "that while we were still sinners, Christ died for us" (Romans 5:8). These Scriptures reveal that God's bountiful love is shown in Christ. This is the God we trust for a harvest—the God who allowed His Son to die so that we may live.

As difficult as it is for us to wrap our minds around, God loves our children far more than we ever could. His hands are far more capable than our own. His vision sees further. His presence goes with us (Exodus 33:14–15). His plans are far more wonderful than our own (Isaiah 55:8–9). We think we know what's best for our children. But our best for them pales in comparison to God's best.

As we grow in knowledge of God, we grow in our love for Him. And as we grow in our love for God, we grow in trust. Slowly, the burdens and fears of motherhood begin to feel lighter. We realize that we are merely coworkers. The growth is His to provide. The harvest is His to gather. More than our children are our own, our children are first and foremost God's.

Feel the uncomfortable jitters of surrendering control. Lift your eyes to the heavens. Grin in the face of uncertainty. Trust that He who promises is faithful (Hebrews 10:23).

And get your hands in the dirt.

Plant seeds of the gospel. Pull the weeds of sin, not only in their hearts but also in your own. Water with the Word of God, which refreshes the soul.

Work heartily unto the Lord and rest at the end of a long day, trusting that growth is the Lord's domain. We can sit back and behold the beauty of God's creation in our children: the way her nose crinkles when she smiles, the way his hair shines golden in the sun, the way that she is steadily grasping the truths of God. *Surely, God is at work.*

Nowadays, I watch my young son run wild and free in those green corn fields that line my grandparents' street. It's springtime—and the fields have a ways to go before harvest. And so does my son, but he's growing taller and more inquisitive by the day. *Surely, God is at work.* Something about watching a growing child play in the growing fields reminds me of those key tenets of farming, tenets that feel as ingrained into God's creation as they are into motherhood—working, waiting, hoping—sewn together in trust. He who promised is faithful.

By God's grace, perhaps I do know a bit about farming—and maybe even a bit about motherhood. Both farmers and mothers must trust in the sovereign plan of the One who causes growth.

Therefore, brothers and sisters, be patient until the Lord's coming. See how the farmer waits for the precious fruit of the earth and is patient with it until it receives the early and the late rains. You also must be patient. Strengthen your hearts, because the Lord's coming is near.

JAMES 5:7–8

This essay was originally published in issue 8 of Gospel at Home™ *magazine.*

Deep as the Ocean, High as the Sky

KATIE DAVIDSON

Mama: "I love you deep as the ocean, high as the sky!"
S: "No, I love YOU deep as the ocean and high as the sky!"
Mama: "But you know who loves even more, right?"
S: "God."
Mama: "Yes, that's right. Good night, my love."

This little conversation happens almost every night at my house. It's one of those small, everyday routines that, for once, feels more meaningful than mundane. I look forward to tomorrow's goodnight exchange just as soon as tonight's is over.

But most of the time, routines are the opposite—they feel more mundane than meaningful. Opening another juice box. Changing another diaper. Cleaning up more Goldfish® caked to the crevices of the car. It's easy to accumulate these mundane moments and chalk them up to a mundane life. It's easy to feel unseen in the constant service. It's easy to live out of lack—a lack of energy, a lack of rest, a lack of time.

How does God's love impact even these mundane moments? Scripture tells us that because of His great love for us, God, who is rich in mercy, made us alive with Christ even when we were dead in sin (Ephesians 2:4–5). God's Word reminds us that His compassion never fails (Lamentations 3:22). Romans 8:38–39 reminds us that nothing (no tantrum, no endless pile of laundry, no harsh word spoken) can separate us from the love of God. As you pour yourself out to your child, God pours His love into you.

So what if we flipped our own script? What if we lived out of the abundance of God's love rather than our lack? What if we mothered out of the truth that God loves us as deep as the ocean and high as the sky?

What I love about Scripture is that it reminds us that we are not alone. Its pages tell the story of mom after mom who is personally and profoundly impacted by God's genuine love for them—how God showed up for them in the everyday feelings and trials of motherhood. In their stories, we can be reminded that His love shows up for us, too.

Let's take a look at three mothers from Scripture—mothers who experienced God's love and faithfulness in their own unique circumstances.

JOCHEBED
A Mother with an Obstacle
Exodus 2:1–10

It's no secret that motherhood comes with decisions. And Jochebed had a difficult decision to make. In a time when the Israelites were enslaved by Pharaoh in Egypt, God blessed His people and multiplied them greatly. Pharoah felt threatened and instructed every Hebrew baby boy to be thrown into the Nile River. But Jochebed took a chance. She hid her beloved son for three months and then, in faith, placed him into a floating basket in the Nile and trusted God with the rest. Sure enough, a daughter of Pharaoh found the boy and adopted him as her son. The boy was saved by his mother's faith. And do you know what this boy's name was? Moses, the deliverer of God's people from Egypt—the man who spoke to God face to face, as one would with a friend (Exodus 33:11).

I can imagine that Jochebed felt enormous fear and anxiety as she hid her son. I can imagine her hands shaking as she placed baby Moses in the river. But the waters intended for death became a means of deliverance.

God honored a mother's faith and taught her that He is the great Caretaker of His children. When we feel exhausted, when we face obstacles that seem too big for us, we can look to Jochebed's story and remember that no obstacles are too big for God. God, in fact, used a criminal's cross to bring hope for His people. And sometimes, even in our own lives, He uses

As you pour yourself out to your child, God pours His love into you.

the hardest of seasons to strengthen our faith and remind us of His love for us, which never fails.

RACHEL

A Mother Fraught with Comparison
Genesis 29-30

Rachel was a beautiful shepherdess who caught the attention of a man named Jacob. This man loved Rachel so much that he was willing to work for her father for seven years to marry her. But her father Laban played a trick on Jacob—under the guise of darkness, Laban gave Jacob Rachel's older sister Leah to marry instead. Jacob consummated his marriage with the wrong woman and agreed to work another seven years to marry Rachel as well. Though Jacob loved Rachel more, only Leah was able to bear him children. Rachel watched her sister become pregnant again and again as she remained barren, constantly reminded of her lack. And though she gave Jacob her servant Bilhah to bear children in her place, these children did not fill the hole in Rachel's heart. She had beauty, and she had Jacob's love, but she wanted the one thing she could not have—her own child.

Yet this was not the end of her story. Redemption comes for Rachel in Genesis 30:22—God remembered Rachel in His love. He listened to her, and Rachel became pregnant with a son of her own—and later, another. Years and years of feeling like she was not enough, years and years of seeing others receive just what she prayed for, changed in a single moment. Rachel was not forgotten. God was not angry with her, nor did He love her any less. God's timing was simply not her own.

Are you in a season of waiting? Are you watching the prayers of other moms get answered? Are you wanting what you cannot seem to have? Remember that God is listening. What great love this is! The God who gives the sea its boundaries, who holds the planets in place, who numbers the hairs on your head, listens intently to each one of your prayers. When you call on God for help, when you are stuck in a rut of comparison, when you feel like you are not enough in the journey of motherhood, remember God hears the prayers of the righteous (Proverbs 15:29), and you have been made righteous by grace through faith in Jesus when you have trusted Him as your Savior.

LOIS AND EUNICE
Mothers Behind the Scenes
Acts 16:1; 2 Timothy 1:5

The truth is, we do not know much about Lois and Eunice except that they were so genuine, so full of integrity, that Paul calls their faith a "sincere faith" (2 Timothy 1:5). They lived out their faith. They conducted their home in a way that honored the Lord.

Who were Lois and Eunice? They were the grandmother and mother of Timothy, Paul's beloved son in the faith. Paul tells us in Acts 16 that Eunice was a Jewish woman who believed in Jesus; she likely came to faith upon Paul's first ministry journey in Lystra. But Eunice faced significant challenges to her faith. Her husband was a Gentile and was never mentioned by Paul as supporting Timothy's faith. And Lystra was not an easy place to be a Christian. Lystra was a small town that was largely unfamiliar with the Jewish God, a small town that was consumed with worship of little "g" gods—so much so that Lystrans believed Paul and Barnabas to be Hermes and Zeus upon their visit (Acts 14:8–20).

Lois and Eunice raised Timothy in a countercultural home where he learned the Scriptures from infancy (2 Timothy 3:15). God honored the women's efforts, for they had the joy of seeing Timothy grow up to love Jesus and be chosen to preach the gospel alongside Paul, eventually carrying on Paul's ministry.

No, we do not have accounts of specific events in the lives of Lois and Eunice, yet we see the profound legacy that a faithful woman can have on the faith of a child. We see the potential of our own lives in Lois and Eunice. We are reminded that everyday faithfulness matters—that teaching our children Scripture matters. We are reminded that in God's sovereign wisdom, He created the family as the perfect training grounds for children to learn and grow in faith. He chose everyday women doing everyday motherly things as a model of His perfect love.

The mundane matters. The love we show our kids by slicing apples or folding the fifth load of laundry this week or praying for them before a big test—that sacrificial love gives them a framework from which to understand the magnitude of God's great love. As you participate in those mundane tasks, as you breathe a sigh of relief as the kids go to bed

*God's love for you stretches
deeper than the ocean
and higher than the sky.*

only to realize it's your own bedtime, God's love for you stretches deeper than the ocean and higher than the sky. God's love for you cannot be measured or calculated. It can't even truly be described. God loved you enough to turn His face away (temporarily) as His own Son hung on the cross so that you could be saved (Matthew 27:46).

God allowed Himself to experience pain that we would never choose for ourselves. Surely, He is faithful in love to His people. And His faithful love endures forever—proven in the person and work of Jesus (Psalm 136). God's love is with you in the sleepless nights, as you break up sibling fights, as you strive to love your kids with all your might. How wonderful, how magnificent, how gigantic is the love of God for mothers. How wonderful, how magnificent, how gigantic is the love of God for you.

This essay was originally published in issue 7 of Gospel at Home™ *magazine.*

Rest for Weary Days
of Motherhood

Rest in the Midst of Our Work

BETH WHITE

Before my daughter, Penelope, was born, I had grand aspirations of traveling with my baby. My husband and I love making regular weekend trips, and we usually take one or two long vacations a year. We purchased a highly-rated travel crib that was light and easy to carry, and we were so excited about introducing our little girl to the joys of vacationing—we even planned to introduce camping into our family traditions.

Penelope is now almost one year old, and despite our best efforts (and the fact that she sleeps through the night every night at home), she will not sleep overnight in her travel crib. We have tried everything, but all our attempts at travel have ended in one of two ways: either my husband or I will stay up with her all night every night, or we will all drive home in the middle of the night. No matter how tired she is, this baby can only find rest in one spot: her own room in her own crib.

We are all a little like my daughter. Just like her tired little body desperately needs sleep, as moms, we all know we desperately need rest. But just like Penelope, there is only one place we can actually find it. Jesus says in Matthew 11:28–30, "Come to me, all of you who are weary and burdened, and I will give you rest. Take my yoke upon you and learn from me, because I am lowly and humble in heart, and you will find rest for your souls. For my yoke is easy and my burden is light."

Being a mother is practically synonymous with being tired. No matter what stage of motherhood you are in—from pregnancy through your children's adulthood—you are almost certainly mentally, emotionally, spiritually, and physically tired. And of course you are! There is a lot to do and a lot to keep track of. Motherhood consumes us and becomes one of our top priorities, if not our top priority.

He is the promised Messiah who has come to restore all things, redeem humanity, and provide true rest.

As moms, we are responsible for keeping our children alive, caring for them emotionally, and teaching them how to function in the world. As Christian moms, we then have a whole other set of responsibilities. We have to teach our children about Jesus and model a life focused on Him. Obviously, not all of this is on us alone—we have family and churches to help us—but the buck typically stops with us and our husbands. It is a lot of pressure, and as a result, we are tired, and we are busy.

But Jesus promises rest. He promises it to *all who are weary and burdened*, and that includes us tired and busy moms. Being a mom does not put our need for rest in Jesus on pause; in fact, it makes our need for His rest more obvious. But how do we rest in Jesus when we are this tired and busy? Where do we find time for prayer and Bible study?

When we cannot find the time and when we feel weary and burdened, we may need to redefine how we think about the rest that Jesus gives us. Rest is not just quiet, still, peaceful, kid-free time with Jesus with a cup of coffee and a clean house. The rest Jesus gives is a constant state of being, and it is found in doing the *work* of the kingdom—as long as that work is being done *with* the King. And the Bible shows us this truth in the passage that follows Matthew 11:28–30.

Immediately after Jesus tells His disciples that all who come to Him will find rest, the Pharisees rebuke Jesus and His disciples because they stop to pick and eat some grain on the Sabbath, which the Pharisees claim is an unlawful thing to do on the day of rest. Yet Jesus defends His disciples, and then He heals a man on the Sabbath and is rebuked for that (Matthew 12:1–14).

While our Bibles have Jesus's teaching about rest (Matthew 11:28–30) and these two accounts of His ministry (Matthew 12:1–14) separated by a chapter break, Matthew likely intended us to read them in light of each other. On the day of rest, Jesus was allowing His disciples to work to feed themselves to fuel their ministry. And He Himself was

Even our work can be restful as long as it is kingdom work done with the King.

working to bring healing on this day because the Sabbath—God's true rest—had come permanently in the person of Jesus.

The Sabbath was given to the Israelites as a day of rest so that they might know it is the Lord who sanctifies them (Ezekiel 20:12). Each week, as they observed the Sabbath, they were in a way practicing what it would be like when God brought sanctification to His people through Christ. So, what Jesus is saying in Matthew 11:28–30 and demonstrating in Matthew 12:1–14 is that He is the promised Messiah who has come to restore all things, redeem humanity, and provide true rest. The Pharisees just expected something different.

As moms, we likely expect rest to look different as well, but what Jesus shows us is that even our work can be restful as long as it is kingdom work done with the King. And believe me, what you do as a mom is kingdom work. Everything you do for your children can point them to Christ. As you nurse them emotionally or physically when they are not feeling well, you are showing them Jesus's compassion (Matthew 20:29–34, John 11:20–27). As you teach them and correct them, you are modeling Jesus's instructions to His disciples (Mark 9:33–37). Even as you feed them and provide nourishment to their bodies, you are demonstrating His care for the nourishment of His followers (Matthew 12:1–8, 14:13–21). All of these seemingly basic aspects of motherhood are ways you are doing the work of the kingdom and fulfilling your ultimate purpose as a follower of Jesus, which is to become more and more conformed to His self-giving love, which absolutely happens as you raise your children.

As we partner with Jesus in the kingdom work of raising our children, let us not lose heart. The beauty of kingdom work is that it is not *our* work, nor is it dependent on us. The Spirit of Christ, who dwells in each follower of Jesus, is the One who produces results, both in us and in our children. He is the source of our strength and our effort, which is how He provides us with rest.

In a funny way, though it can be frustrating at times when my daughter refuses to find rest anywhere but in her own crib, this small example reminds me that I, too, can only find true rest in one place—rather, in one Person. Of course, I am not referring to my nightly sleep routine; I am referring to the rest that Christ provides—the rest that ultimately nourishes my weary soul. So, as we go about our tired and busy days of motherhood, may we all remember this truth: our true rest is only found in our King, Jesus Christ.

*Everything you do for your children
can point them to Christ.*

This essay was originally published in issue 5 of Gospel at Home™ *magazine.*

When Our Roles Don't
Feel Like "Enough"

JILL ROHRBAUGH

Do you ever wake up in the morning feeling *purposeless*?

Me too…especially when the week has been tough, and life feels mundane.

Recently, I've been really praying to the Lord about wanting to feel excited again when I wake up and look at motherhood with satisfaction and contentment. I think when we are young, we automatically dream big with great expectancy, and then we get older, and our vision seems to slowly narrow. As women, we often have big dreams for either careers or getting married and having kids, and for many of us, *it's both.* Then, not long after we get married and have kids or get the career we've always dreamed of, it seems we hit the "peak" of our lives. And once the honeymoon phase is over (not just with our husbands but the whole daydream we grew up with), we find ourselves saying, "Now what?"

Right now, for me, it's *wake up, dishes, feed kids, homeschool, pick up toys, make lunch, nap time, pick up toys, make dinner, clean up dinner, baths, pick up toys, bed.* Of course, there are exciting things that we do every now and then, like date nights and special events. And we still hope and dream about things, like going on vacation and maybe having a beach house of our own or a new business venture one day. But that's not the dream or vision we've waited for our whole lives, ya know? And we can feel, kind of, well…*stuck.*

So how do we feel excited again? That's what I had been asking the Lord. Through Scripture, devotions, and other sources, the word "worship" kept coming up. Consistently, I was being reminded that my purpose was to worship and glorify Him.

Psalm 148:3–5 (ESV) says: "Praise him, sun and moon, praise him, all you shining stars! Praise him, you highest heavens, and you waters above the heavens! Let them praise the name of the LORD! For he commanded and they were created."

To praise Him is to worship Him. And when you think about the purpose of the sun, moon, and stars, it's for people to see them and see God and His goodness. So if that's what His creation's purpose is, then isn't it ours too? And how do we do that in the mundane?

When I really began to meditate on that, things started to change. Specifically, my perspective changed. I realized that when I feed my children, I show them God as a provider. When I hug them, I glorify God as a comforter. When I listen to them speak, I show them that God hears us. When I clean and organize my home, I show them that God brings order to things. When I discipline them lovingly, I show them that God does the same. Every single moment of each day is my opportunity to show my children who God is. Every task that is set before me is my chance to glorify God and how amazing He is. How beautiful the role of a wife, a mom, and a woman! How can I not be excited when I look at it this way? My purpose becomes clear, and my tasks no longer seem mundane but extremely worthy and important.

Below is a prayer that I have started to pray when I wonder about my purpose. I encourage you to pray it, too.

Lord, whenever my mind starts to believe that my tasks are mundane and unimportant, remind me what a privilege it is to show others who You are. The journey of my life is not a goal to be reached or a success to achieve but simply to glorify and worship the goodness that is YOU. Let all lies from the enemy be far from me, and let me live by this truth — that if the stars were made to worship, then so am I. In Jesus's name, Amen.

This essay was originally published in issue 1 of Gospel at Home™ *magazine.*

*Every single moment of
each day is my opportunity to
show my children who God is.*

Enough Already

ANNE IMBODEN

Last week my ten-year-old hopped in the car after school and proceeded to give me a rundown of the day's events. Usually, it's pretty standard stuff: quizzes she took, what she chose for lunch, the newest skill she's learning in P.E., or sometimes petty drama she witnesses between friends. But on this particular day, Providence said, "I think my English teacher was having a hard day today." When I asked what made her say that, she said matter of factly, "Well, when we came back to homeroom, Mrs. K was sitting at her desk. The lights were off and . . . she had a bucket on her head."

I looked up at my daughter through the rearview mirror. "Seriously?" Prov just shrugged and said, "Ya, I think she'd just had enough and needed a dark, quiet space." My heart went out to dear Mrs. K. I wondered how long she'd been under there. Poor thing. "Well, some days are just like that, especially for teachers," I said. "Did you say anything to her?" Prov replied, "I went up to her and gently tapped on the bucket and asked her if she was okay. She said she just needed a minute." I nodded in understanding. That night, my daughter looked up Bible verses and wrote them out for her teacher, hoping to give her some encouragement. Bless her heart.

I can only imagine what went down in a fourth-grade English class that caused a capable, smart, perfectly sane woman to sit in total darkness and don a bucket over her head. As far as coping mechanisms go, it's pretty brilliant, don't you think?

We've all had days (or years—I'm looking at you, 2020) when we just can't cope anymore—days when we just have to say, "Enough already." What can we do when we reach our wits' end? Tempting as it is, we can't very well shut out the world and retreat. We have people counting on us. We have expectations to meet, duties to fulfill, families to care for, and showers to take. (I threw that last one in there for good measure because, let's be real, sometimes the bar just needs to be lowered on hard days.) We can go for a walk, take a nap, escape into a good book for a while, sit out on the porch with a beverage of our choice, or call a friend or a therapist. But first, it's important to understand what brought us to the end of our rope.

I'm certain I'm not the only parent who finds themselves saying, "That's enough!" to their children (usually in a shrill, strained voice that borders on psychotic). I've had enough of the bickering, enough of the back talk, enough of the eye-rolling, enough of the snarkiness, enough of the whining. Pick your poison; there's always something. "Enough,"[1] by simple definition, means to have as much or as many as required (thank you, Merriam-Webster). So really, what we're saying when we've had enough, be it our children's bad attitude or a decadent dessert, is that we can't handle anymore. We don't need it. We don't want it. Our tanks are full (often not in a good way), and any bit more will cause us to overflow, snap, or lose our ever-loving minds.

Enough is, well, enough. It's a declaration, a hand held up in resistance to any more. It's a bucket over our heads, sending a clear message that we've *had* it. But it's also a question, isn't it? Haven't you ever asked yourself: *Did I do enough? Am I contributing enough? Am I smart enough? Do I have enough? Am I strong enough? Am I brave enough? Is there enough time? Am I enough?* I'm willing to bet the weight of at least one of those questions is what's led us to our own under-a-bucket moments.

I could fill pages with examples of times when I questioned whether or not I was enough: for my husband, my kids, or my friends. I lacked the strength, the patience, the energy, the giftedness, or the time. I didn't have enough of any of those things. The pressure I've felt to be everything to everyone has been enormous, so much so that just one more straw would break my back. A phone call from the school nurse, a slow-moving six-year-old during the morning rush, or a last-minute request from a friend could have me reaching for the bucket and saying, "Nope. Can't do it. I've had enough." In those moments, we need to remember that what we lack in patience, God has in spades. When our strength falls short, God's strength prevails. When our fear feels paralyzing, God steadily leads us on. When we don't have enough, He does, always. Unlike us, God has no limits. His wits have no end, and neither do His mercies.

Sometimes, we need to step away for a minute. My kids will tell you I do this often. I just need to regroup and pull myself together before I say or do something totally un-Christlike. (Okay, full disclosure: sometimes I walk away because I've done something un-Christlike, and I have to check my heart and swallow a big dose of humility before returning to the table. This happens often, too. As in, this morning.)

It's okay to clock out if it helps you. Turn the lights off and duck under a bucket (or whatever "clocking out" looks like for you). But might I suggest you do some praying while you're under there? You may be familiar with 1 Peter 5:7, which says, "casting all your cares on him, because he cares about you." This verse is comforting, and it's true. But the verse preceding it shouldn't be missed. "Humble yourselves," it begins, "therefore, under the mighty hand of God, so that he may exalt you at the proper time" (verse 6). Before we unload our worries, our burdens, or whatever it is that's led us to throw our arms up in the air and say, "Enough," we must begin with humility. We need to start by admitting we don't have enough to be everything to everyone or to do it all. We can't offload the weight we carry without first confessing we trust Him to carry it for us because we're just not capable on our own. Bottom line? We are not enough, not without God.

In 2 Corinthians 12, the Apostle Paul describes struggling with "a thorn in the flesh" that was given to him. He describes this as "a messenger of Satan to torment me so that I would not exalt myself," and he says, "Concerning this, I pleaded with the Lord three times that it would leave me" (verses 7–8). I can't speak to what Paul was dealing with exactly, but I can certainly relate to that "thorn in my flesh" feeling. For teachers, it may be a particular student. (Calling them a "messenger of Satan" seems a little severe, but we all know every class has that *one* kid who makes you wonder from which realm they were sent.) It may be a coworker, a family member, a professor, or something else altogether that constantly pushes your buttons and shoves you right up to the brink of your sanity. God's response to Paul's struggle is what we all need to hear: "But he said to me, 'My grace is sufficient for you, for my power is perfected in weakness'" (verse 9). "Sufficient" is just a fancy word for "enough," and God's grace is just that: it is as much as we require. It's *all* we require.

So before you place that bucket over your head, flip it over and dump out all your frustrations, anger, anxiety, and fear. Give it a good shake. Next, turn it back over and imagine it's been filled to the brim with God's grace. Then gently overturn that bucket and set it over your head like a crown. Let His grace wash over you. Sit humbled in the dark, quiet space and know you have enough to get through.

Unlike us, God has no limits.
His wits have no end,
and neither do His mercies.

This essay was originally published in issue 1 of Gospel at Home™ *magazine.*

Peaceful Chaos: An Oxymoron or the Way of Grace?

COLLEEN WACHOB

It is a quiet morning. Soft light is just beginning to break over the desert hills. From my worn white and blue paisley chair, I watch faint clouds streaking across the grayish sky. My Bible and journal are open in my lap, and beside me, a fir-scented candle, leftover from Advent, flickers. Steam rises from my cup of milky tea. And I am at peace, my heart settled before the Lord.

It is easy to feel at peace when our external worlds are still: When my family circles the dinner table without any squabbles erupting over where to sit or whose hand isn't clean enough to hold as we bow to pray together. When my house sparkles with just-scrubbed cleanliness as I sit back to enjoy the gentle order of things. When I run in the softness of a new day as my sneaker-shod feet pound a rhythm of peace into the pavement. When we pitch our tent in the mountains and breathe in the glory and beauty of the wilderness.

But for every moment of perfect, soul-quieting tranquility, there are countless moments of mess. Of frazzle. Of abject chaos. Of war. So, what about those moments? When my five girls bicker over pencils and hair ties and who borrowed whose shoes without asking. When the house is a helter-skelter, all-over disaster of toys and LEGO® bricks and clothes and unwashed dishes. When there are too many tasks and too many places to be and my well-laid plans unravel in the face of unexpected needs. When evil strikes a world away—or even down the street—and the atrocities break my heart in pieces. When we hear of war. Of conflict and hatred and brokenness. When disaster crashes over us or the diagnosis is grim or the bank account is empty. Where is peace in those moments?

As a mom, this has been my constant battle. How can my heart be at peace even when the world around me is utter chaos—either the small world inside the walls of my home or outside in the vast cosmos inhabited by millions of other people just as broken as I am? All of us long for peace. For joy. And as Christians, we know that true peace is only found through Jesus Christ. But, often, we cling to circumstantial peace, to external peace, and then find ourselves despondent or frustrated when those fleeting moments vanish. We are prone to distress, anxiety, and even anger when the peace we crave is dashed by either a toy room explosion or a global news report.

By modern definition, peace refers to the absence of war or conflict. It involves those in disagreement coming together. Peace also refers to rest, calm, and tranquility; we might say that a warm day on the beach is *peaceful* or that the still quiet of the forest fills our hearts with peace. But the biblical definition of peace goes beyond what we read in the dictionary.

According to Strong's Concordance, the root meaning of the Hebrew word *shalom*[2] is "completeness" or "soundness." It implies a fullness that has no deficiency. The Greek word for peace, *eiréné*[3], is defined as "oneness, quietness, and rest." In the beginning, when the world was new, our God of peace dwelled in perfect *shalom* with His created beings. He walked with Adam and Eve in the beautiful, orderly garden, where every need was met in fullness, and there was no deficiency in relationship, no lack, no brokenness. But, when sin entered the world, that serene, beautiful, and utterly complete peace shattered. The world—and human hearts—became broken. God, who is unchanging, was not surprised by the unraveling of the peaceful world He had formed. And He began to weave a breathtaking story of sacrifice and redemption and *peace* restored.

Isaiah 9:6 foreshadows the coming of Jesus Christ, calling Him the "Prince of Peace." And we see Jesus fulfilling this prophecy through His death on the cross. Romans 5:1 says, "Therefore, since we have been justified by faith, we have peace with God through our Lord Jesus Christ." Ephesians 2:14 says, "For he is our peace, who made both groups one and tore down the dividing wall of hostility." And on Jesus's last night with the disciples, He promised His peace, saying, "Peace I leave with you. My peace I give to you. I do not give to you as the world gives. Don't let your heart be troubled or fearful" (John 14:27).

Peace is a supernatural gift from God—the peace we have with God through the atonement and mediation of Jesus Christ, the peace we can enjoy in fellowship with others as we experience like-minded unity, and the peace we have within ourselves because our souls have found rest in God alone (Psalm 62:1). I am cognitively certain of these truths. But cognitive certainty doesn't always flow seamlessly into experience, does it?

Furthermore, we know that, as Christians, we should have peace. Galatians 5:22 lists peace among the fruit of the Spirit. The Holy Spirit works in us to yield the fruit of peace—demonstrating that peace is not merely a circumstantial feeling but a trait of godliness. In Matthew 5:9, Jesus says, "Blessed are the peacemakers, for they shall be called sons of God." Peace-dwelling, peace-making, peace-living—all of these aspects of inward and outward peace are clearly a part of our calling as believers. But how?

Understanding peace as completion in Christ enables us to establish our hearts in peace, to settle them and root them deeply and unalterably in His work on the cross. If I grasp whole-heartedly that Christ is the source of my peace—both internally and externally—I am anchored firmly against the storms that batter my sails. When chaos erupts, I can breathe a soft prayer of surrender, recognizing that this moment of mayhem has been sifted down to me through God's kind and gentle fingers. I can choose to glorify God by responding with grace. I can believe that God has given me everything I need, both practically and emotionally, for this "thing" and all things.

Philippians 4 holds gems of truth for us frazzled humans as we wrestle for peace and joy in a messy world. Verses 6 and 7 say, "Don't worry about anything, but in everything, through prayer and petition with thanksgiving, present your requests to God. And the peace of God, which surpasses all understanding, will guard your hearts and minds in Christ Jesus." Unshakable peace begins with gratitude. If God has graciously given us all things, then we can rest contentedly in our circumstances with thankful hearts. When my children bicker with one another, I can say, "Thank You, Lord, for this opportunity to train these precious hearts in Your ways. Please guide me and give me patience." When my living room is an explosion of "stuff," I can pray, "Thank You for this home and the constancy of Your provision. You are so good to us. Help us steward Your gifts well." And when a broken foot keeps me from running or chasing my children, I can say, "God, thank You for this body and the miracle of how it works. I wouldn't have written this injury into my story, but I trust that You want to shape my heart through this trial. Help me draw near to You."

The Apostle Paul begins each of his New Testament letters with a greeting of peace. As a wonderful former pastor of mine used to say in his warm Southern drawl, "Paul always starts with grace and peace," and this is where we should begin as well. Enemies of God in our sin, we received grace and mercy at the cross. Jesus's death on the cross became the way of peace, the means to reconciliation with our Maker. Now at peace with God, our hearts knit together with His, we can be at peace with each other. We can extend grace, understanding, kindness, and forbearance to one another. We can choose the way of peacemaking instead of grappling to prove ourselves. And we can have hearts at rest in God's goodness so that we bring a spirit of peacefulness with us wherever we go, blessing and encouraging those we encounter along the way.

Lord, I pray that You would establish Your peace in
our hearts so that we might extend peace to others.
Thank You for the peace You came to bring.

"May the Lord of peace himself give you peace always
in every way. The Lord be with all of you."

2 THESSALONIANS 3:16

This essay was originally published in issue 29 of Be Still Magazine®.

Peace is a supernatural gift from God.

Stocking Up in Christ

ANNA ELIZABETH TAYLOR

About a year ago, a string of headlines ignited a familiar panic in me.

"Infant Formula Out of Stock"

"Baby Aisle Shelves Empty"

My news alerts might as well say, "Your Baby Will Not Get What He Needs." As a brand-new mom, my instinct is to fight "mama bear style"—protect my family, stock up for my little one, and throw elbows in the grocery store. It's an instinct to put myself first, hoard the limited resources I can, and strive for security in a few extra cans of formula. It's a "nesting" instinct I can justify when providing for my six-month-old.

Truthfully though, that hoarding instinct is all too familiar. That's the feeling I had while buying toilet paper and Lysol wipes at the start of the pandemic. *Me first, me first.* That's the desire to buy a big house and stock all the cupboards. *I need this.* That's the reassurance I look for while checking my bank statement. *This will keep me safe.*

A supply shortage may highlight a particular type of selfishness in hoarding, but what does the Bible say about "stocking up" in general? Mark 6:8–9 describes Jesus's directions to His apostles: "He instructed them to take nothing for the road except a staff—no bread, no traveling bag, no money in their belts, but to wear sandals and not put on an extra shirt." In Matthew 6:11, Jesus prays a similar plea: "Give us today our daily bread," which echoes God's directions for His people in Exodus 16:

"The people are to go out each day and gather *enough for that day*" (verse 4, emphasis added).

In each of these scenarios, God's people are instructed to limit their resources. A picture is coming into focus of how disciples of Jesus should live, but is that the whole picture? As Christians, should we be against full cupboards and stocked closets? Should we be focusing on each day rather than preparing for the future? Where would Jesus be among the grocery lines and superstore aisles (maybe turning water into precious formula!)?

REMOVE FROM CART: ANXIOUS STRIVING

Continuing in Mark 6, a stark contrast is immediately offered. While Jesus sent the apostles out with nothing but hiking sticks and sandals, Herod threw a party to impress. Attempting to satiate every desire and gain approval through material things, Herod promised his wife's daughter up to half the kingdom (Mark 6:23). When platters full of lavish food did not satisfy, Herod's family instead demanded John the Baptist's head to be served up on those platters. With seemingly every resource at their disposal, they still sought after true contentment, resorting to revenge, violence, and shock.

The extreme comparison conveys a critical warning: If you're not willing to leave your possessions and follow Jesus, you may be walking a tiresome road of striving and dissatisfaction. You may be leaning on fleeting wealth or privilege for security. Haggai 1:6 reminds me of Herod's toils: "You have planted much but harvested little. You eat but never have enough to be satisfied. You drink but never have enough to be happy. You put on clothes but never have enough to get warm. The wage earner puts his wages into a bag with a hole in it." Herod trusted in his riches for security and acceptance... and they were not enough.

STOCK UP ON: SECURITY IN CHRIST

The picture becomes clearer. If we find our security in material abundance, we will always be striving. If we seek satisfaction in worldly things, we will never know rest. Instead, the gospel declares our security and satisfaction are in Christ alone. When we recognize our inability to save ourselves—physically and spiritually—we find a deep comfort in the Lord's promises.

Then, while those around us shout and struggle in a frenzy of need, we remain rooted in Christ (Colossians 2:7). When our stockpiles expire and our supply chains jam, we remain secure in our salvation. As Christians, whether we choose to buy extra groceries or not, our hope is no longer in our hoarding but in our heavenly home.

REMOVE FROM CART: ISOLATING GREED

Finding hope and security in Christ frees Christians from burdensome striving. At the same time, it drives us to be more like Christ in all we do. So the question remains: Is stocking up on food and supplies Christlike?

When resources are sparse, the selfish tendency to safeguard with extra "stuff" is more evident *and* more problematic. After all, the command to "love your neighbor" is certainly woven throughout Scripture and displayed in Jesus's life. And how can I love my neighbors while taking more than what I need and leaving them with less? Truly, an ugly, self-centered, merciless greed emerges when I pit myself against others for supplies.

Usually, though, it doesn't feel selfish to buy three boxes of cereal at once, barely reducing the stock of a typically full grocery aisle. Who am I hurting in this act of preparation and convenience?

"Stocking up" may not always be greedy or unkind, but it can lead to an isolating independence. I may ask fewer favors of my neighbors *and* be less likely to offer help when they need it. I may fall into a trap of thinking, "I bought these extras so that I have them *when I need them*," or "I can't spare my time or money when there's so much to prepare for *my own future*." My focus on stockpiling may prevent me from acting in generosity toward others or thankfulness toward the Lord. I may even be too anxious to enjoy the resources I do have. Indeed, God calls the man who spends his whole life accumulating possessions for himself a fool (Luke 12:20).

STOCK UP ON: GENEROSITY IN COMMUNITY

Instead, if we stock up on supplies in order to love our neighbors *better*, we have an opportunity to be "rich toward God" (Luke 12:21) with our resources. As we give more away, we may even be given more as Proverbs 11:24 explains: "One person gives freely, yet gains more."

Buying in bulk may allow us to bless our neighbors with resources now. Alternatively, it may free our time to more easily bless others with our presence later. If we buy extra items but hold them with a loose grip for those in need, we can be generous on demand. If having spare cans of kidney beans in the cupboard makes it easier to invite someone over for chili after church, buy those beans!

Finally, notice that greedy motives can hinder the blessings of both giving and receiving in community. In Mark 6, Jesus doesn't directly command the apostles to be generous *toward* others, but He does presuppose a reliance *on* others. Just as God provided manna for His people in Exodus, so would the new Christian community care for Christ's disciples each day. God asks us to put aside our pride and autonomy—characteristics that often accompany hoarding—to better glorify Him in community. Our dependence on Christ can often overflow into a humble dependence on others.

As the baby formula headlines whirled around, I felt God's tangible care for me through His loving Church. Attending a mom's group full of advice and receiving texts from out-of-state friends wanting to help, I saw the full impact of a far-reaching community that cares for my baby like family. I am thankful for shared resources and packages of our hypoallergenic formula, but I am also thankful for the prayers and encouragement of this family of believers. In what could have been a time of struggle, stress, and selfishness, I felt cared for and confident in the community of Christ.

In the end, having extra supplies on hand can be helpful, but we must not be tricked into thinking we can "do it on our own" because only the hope of Christ brings lasting security. Filled with that assurance, we are then able to overflow generously as a picture of Christ to our neighbors. At the same time, we are reminded of Christ's love for us as we humbly rely on the community of Christ rather than ourselves and our stockpiles.

This essay was originally published in issue 1 of Gospel at Home™ *magazine.*

The gospel declares our security and satisfaction are in Christ alone.

It Won't Always Be This Hard

CASSIE WHITMAN

I see you. I see you stepping on the blocks you asked to be picked up twelve times already, yelling in both pain and frustration. I see you gradually losing your patience as you practically bribe your kids to "just pick something" when discussing breakfast, lunch, and snack options. I see you boil over in anger as you tell your child for the last time that they need to listen, to stop arguing, to obey, to just do what they are told the first time, over and over and over again.

I am you.

You are not alone in this struggle. You are not alone in these feelings. You are not alone in the breakdown that comes after you finally put your kids to bed and are left in the chaos and mess as you sink to the floor in tears and regret at the way you handled it all today.

You are not alone.

I also see you trying. I see you trying to give your children everything they both need and want. I see you trying to pray and be calm instead of losing it again. I see you trying your best to rely on God for guidance and strength as you learn to love and discipline your children in a godly way. I see you trying...

I am trying, too.

Motherhood is hard. Parenting is hard. Being a godly example for your children is hard, too. Thankfully, we have the best Father figure imaginable. We can look to the cross to remember that truth. God sent His Son, not only to die for our sins and bring us reconciliation with

Him (Romans 5:10) but to give us an example to turn to in all that we do (Philippians 2:6–8, Colossians 3:12–16).

Take a few moments and open your Bible with me as we look at a few passages in Scripture that we can turn to when we face those hard moments, not only in motherhood but in all of life.

ISAIAH 41:10

Do not fear, for I am with you; do not be afraid, for I am your God. I will strengthen you; I will help you; I will hold on to you with my righteous right hand.

When we are in the throes of toddler tantrums, teenage breakdowns, and general childhood stubbornness, we can stop and turn to God. He is with us, He will strengthen us, He will help us, and best of all, He will uphold us with His righteous hand. How great a Father we have!

PSALM 46:1–5

God is our refuge and strength, a helper who is always found in times of trouble. Therefore we will not be afraid, though the earth trembles and the mountains topple into the depths of the seas, though its water roars and foams and the mountains quake with its turmoil. Selah

There is a river — its streams delight the city of God, the holy dwelling place of the Most High. God is within her; she will not be toppled. God will help her when the morning dawns.

When we think we are in too deep — when the troubles and trials come and motherhood is seemingly beating us down blow by blow — we can remember that God is our refuge and strength and help in trouble. He is in the midst of the tantrums, the fights, the disobedience, and our own frustration and anger. With our Father at the center of our trials, we cannot be moved.

EXODUS 14:14

The LORD will fight for you, and you must be quiet.

After bedtime finally rolls around, when the house is quiet (maybe it's still a chaotic mess from the day) and I sit in silence, my thoughts and the guilt and regret from the day set in. Maybe you can relate to these feelings: *I am a bad mom. I shouldn't have lost my temper. Why can't I fix my heart on the right things and be slow to anger? I know "so-and-so" would never yell at her kids.* And the list can go on and on. But friends, God will fight for us! We must go to Him in prayer, confess these sins of anger and lack of self-control, and ask God to move us to look like Christ. We can ask Him to give us opportunities for patience, self-control, and slow and low voices.

God may not simply hand out patience and obedience as an instant cure for our sinful nature, but He will give us opportunities to rely on Him and the Scriptures to act out that patience. In order to hear Him, we must be in the Word. He will fight for us; we need only be silent and listen to His voice.

PHILIPPIANS 4:5–7

Let your graciousness be known to everyone. The Lord is near. Don't worry about anything, but in everything, through prayer and petition with thanksgiving, present your requests to God. And the peace of God, which surpasses all understanding, will guard your hearts and minds in Christ Jesus.

Lastly, when things get hard—when our worries, fears, and anxieties over our parenting and children's futures rise—we can remember the words of Paul. Do not be anxious about anything, but by prayer and petition, let your requests be known to God. He is our Abba Father, and He wants to hear from you! He wants to hear your struggles. He wants to hear your failures, your sins, your temptations, your worries, and your discontentedness. He invites us to commune with Him through prayer. Yes, He already knows what's going on, but He still wants us to come to Him. And when we do, He will grant us His peace, which surpasses all of our understandings, and He will guard our hearts and minds in Jesus.

Friends, when the days are long; the fights seem endless; and repeated disobedience, stubbornness, and tantrums knock us down over and over—don't forget your Father. Turn your eyes to Jesus as your example. Apologize when you lash out, ask for forgiveness from the Father, and pray. The Lord is our refuge, He is our strength, and He is in the midst of this journey of motherhood. It won't always be this hard.

This essay was originally published in issue 4 of Gospel at Home™ *magazine.*

Crying over Spilled Milk

KRISTYN PEREZ

They say not to cry over spilled milk, but I have.

When my kids were little, there were expert mess-makers. As soon as I cleaned up a bin of toys, they'd pour them out. If I went to the bathroom, they'd try to climb on the kitchen table—or worse, into the dryer. The normal exhaustion of motherhood paired with an international move, purchasing cars, and finding housing had finally caught up to me. I was tired, and when one of my little ones spilled her cup of milk, it was enough to bring me to tears.

Recognizing my exhaustion, I often tried to work harder. Maybe if the house wasn't so messy, I wouldn't be so stressed. Maybe if I could get up earlier or have a little more alone time, I wouldn't feel so anxious and worn out. Unfortunately, doing such things could not satisfy my deep weariness. I knew that the Lord was supposed to be my rest, but I was tired and unsure how to practically cling to those promises in this season.

Around this time, I read a psalm that made me both laugh and cry in exhaustion. It says, "Unless the LORD builds a house, its builders labor over it in vain; unless the LORD watches over a city, the watchman stays alert in vain. In vain you get up early and stay up late, working hard to have enough food—yes, he gives sleep to the one he loves" (Psalm 127:1–2).

Well, . . . I remember laughing, . . . *that sounds nice. I would love to get some sleep, but how is all this stuff going to get done? Is God going to clean my house and feed my children in the middle of the night?* I didn't know how to let the Lord "build the house" in this tiring season.

And yet, as I read the words of this psalm over and over, they pierced my heart. I had been laboring hard, trying to serve my husband and children well. I had been trying to "rise up early" and "stay up late" so that I could make my life easier—but still, I was exhausted. And lest I think that early motherhood didn't apply to this kind of rest, I noticed that the next few verses specifically mentioned kids. The psalmist continues to call children a heritage from the Lord and compares them to arrows in the hand of a warrior (Psalm 127:3–4). He even says, "Happy is the man who has filled his quiver with them" (Psalm 127:5).

My tired body didn't miss the irony of these words. God talks about sleep in the same psalm that He mentions having kids. I don't know about you, but I wouldn't link those things together. If you have kids, you usually sleep less. I consistently get less sleep due to the bad dreams and "I can't sleeps" of my children. And yet, God in His sovereignty put these ideas next to one another in a psalm about building and rest.

Throughout Scripture, we are all called to "build." We are given specific ways to love and serve those around us, and being a mom is one of the greatest blessings of my life. But although we are commanded to build, labor, and work hard, all of this work is in vain if not done through the sustaining grace and power of God. Raising children is another form of building, and I can build with my own strength or with the strength the Lord provides. It is in the small, unnoticed moments of the day that God invites me to find His true and abiding rest—rest that is not dependent on my circumstances but on the enduring Word of God.

I love being a mom. I love morning snuggles, kissing "boo-boos," and watching my kids grow and explore the world. I love watching their minds grasp the stories of the Bible in a fresh and childlike way. They sit in awe as they hear that God can turn five loaves of bread and two fish into a feast for thousands of people. Sharing these stories with them helps me to recapture some of the awe and wonder in faith that I've lost with time.

And yet, motherhood is tiring, and there is no quick fix or Band-Aid verse to instant soul rest. God's work is not done in a microwave but through the enduring work of His Word. In tiring seasons, it can be easy to forget the essentials of our faith. We stop meditating on God's Word, we pray less. But if I am not connected to the vine, I produce no good fruit, for apart from Him I can do nothing (John 15:1, 5).

Being a mom has shown me that I am completely dependent on the Lord. So when the milk spills (again) and my temper starts to rise, I can ask for His help. In the day-to-day moments when I am playing building blocks, cleaning the house, reading bedtime stories, or giving baths, He is there. I can sleep well at night, not replaying my anxious thoughts but entrusting them to an all-powerful and all-loving Father. God has offered us a deep rest for our souls as He takes care of us.

—————

God's work is not done in a microwave but through the enduring work of His Word.

—————

This essay was originally published in August 2019 on The Daily Grace® Blog.

God has offered us
a deep rest for our souls
as He takes care of us.

Seeing God in Sickness

KATIE DAVIDSON

"Why, Oh Lord!"

Have you ever prayed this prayer?

Shrouded by lamp-light, I rocked my three-month-old daughter and peered down at my phone. It was 3:00 a.m. Another hour had passed, but she still couldn't sleep. She was weak and wheezing, her eyes red with exhaustion. Her little body was fighting RSV.

She was tired, and so was I. And I thought to myself: *How does God meet me here, right in this moment as a weary mom holding a weary baby? How does His love cradle me as I cradle her in my arms?*

I mulled over this question in my mind and reminded myself of a few truths—truths that I know and yet am forever learning, truths that I pray you can cling to alongside me.

When your family is battling illness, here are three things to remember about God to get you through:

GOD IS SOVEREIGN

Tissues pile up. Cheeks flame red. The days seem long, and you wonder, *When will this end?* In the trenches of motherhood, especially when caring for sick kids, it's easy to feel out of control. The truth is, we are. But we serve a God who is fully in control. God is sovereign over every cough and every upset tummy, every doctor visit and unexpected trip to the ER. There is nothing that happens in our day-to-day lives that is outside His control. Colossians 1:16–17 describes God's sovereignty in this way: "For everything was created by him, in heaven and on earth, the visible and the invisible, whether thrones or dominions or rulers or authorities—all things have been created through him and for him. He is before all things, and by him all things hold together." Nothing surprises God, for it is through Him that all things were created and are sustained. Therefore, when we wake up at 3 a.m., hurting for our feverish babies, we can remember that God cares for our little ones just as He cares for the birds of the sky and the lilies of the field (Matthew 6:26–30 ESV).

GOD IS MY COMFORTER

As we comfort our children, we must remember that we, too, have a Comforter. In fact, Psalm 46 describes God as our refuge and strength, a helper who is always found in times of trouble. When we are weary from another sleepless night, we must remember that our God is with us in every stumbling step to the crib. He has given us Christ Jesus to empathize with us, One who felt human weakness like we do. He has given us His Word to treasure in our hearts so that we may be encouraged and strengthened. And He has given us the Holy Spirit, called the Comforter or Counselor, to teach us the things of God and remind us of His love (John 14:26). God is not simply a deity who observes our actions from afar, but rather, He is a God who comes close. He does not turn away from His weary child. He offers exactly what you need: peace that comes from Him (John 14:27).

GOD IS MY HEAVENLY FATHER

And finally, as you care for your littles, remember you are a mother with a good, good Father in heaven. God listens to you (1 John 5:14). He cares for you (Matthew 7:7–11). He leads you on the right path for His name's sake (Psalm 23:3). He protects you and guides you (Psalm 23:4). He delights in you (Psalm 18:19). Therefore, bring your exhaustion and your weariness before His throne. Bring your joy before His throne. And be encouraged that He delights in you even more so than you delight in your littles.

He is your good Father, and He is also the good Father of your children. As crazy as it seems, God loves your kids more than you do. God's care of your children is better than the care you could ever provide.

Therefore, we can trust in His plan for our kids today and every day. Though He may lead them (and you) through a valley of hardship, He is with them—pursuing their hearts as He pursued yours. And through your tender care and love, He is teaching them a framework through which to understand His tender care and love.

I think back to that night; my daughter was sick with RSV, and I was sick with worry. My heart ached for her. I longed for her body to be healed. I wished I could somehow take the sickness away from her. I wished I could be sick in her place.

And suddenly it hit me. *Maybe this is how God felt, peering down at a world sick with sin.*

His heart ached. He longed for sin to reign no more—for His Creation to be whole and joyful and thriving, as He created it to be.

As I longed for my baby to be healed, how much more did God long for the healing of His people?

And so God did what we wish we could do for our kids: He took the pain upon Himself. Jesus descended from heaven to take on the world's sickness called sin—to bear its consequence upon His shoulders and heal the hearts of God's people forevermore.

As we battle germs and sickness in our homes, as we wipe runny noses and hold fever-stricken children, we can ponder upon the love of God, which is somehow infinitely stronger than the love we feel for our children.

God's care of your children
is better than the care
you could ever provide.

This essay was originally published in January 2024 on The Daily Grace® Blog.

When Kids Cling: Biblical Wisdom for Touched-Out Parents

JACKIE FOSTER

It was one of those rare sunny days in Seattle that was just too good to waste indoors. My baby was sitting up now, and I couldn't wait for him to explore the grass and soak up the gentle sunshine. Imagine my surprise when he twisted around to cling to me for dear life, hoisting his roly-poly legs nearly parallel to his body to avoid touching the grass. *What in the world?* I thought. *The grass isn't going to impale you, kid!* When I took him for his first dip in Lake Washington, it happened again. Up went the legs, and his arms grabbed me with a bearlike strength I wasn't expecting.

SENSORY OVERLOAD

When faced with a new experience, babies often cling — desperately seeking the steady reassurance of being held. Too much sensory input — like from fresh-cut grass, chilly lakewater, or being passed around from auntie to auntie at a family reunion — can easily overstimulate babies and reduce them to tears.

While we might expect babies to respond poorly to sensory overload, we may not consider how we as parents can also become overwhelmed by too much sensory input. If you've ever nursed a hair-pulling infant with razor-sharp fingernails all day while a toddler is wrapped around your leg vying for your attention, you might understand the feeling. Touched-out parents are all too familiar with children who could be described as clingers, crazies, or constants.

CLINGERS, CRAZIES, AND CONSTANTS

Some kids are naturally clingers—and they never seem to grow out of their clinginess. As newborns, they insist on being held nonstop. As toddlers, they often "forget" how to walk. Their kindergarten teachers peel them off you on the first day of school. They cling at playdates and Sunday school drop-off or when it's bath time, bedtime, or any other normal separation point in your day. Constant clinging is enough to leave even the most tenderhearted parents touched out.

Then there are the crazies—a group that the parents of restless school-age children know all too well. Kids who are out of their routines in the summertime and bursting with boundless energy may frequently seek connection—or relief from boredom—through touch. They want to wrestle, roughhouse, pillow-fight, or pelt you with foam darts. They follow you around, beg for your physical presence in their activities, and edge into your personal space while you're cooking or working from home until they're practically (or literally!) sitting on you.

Finally, there are kids who could be categorized as constants. Maybe you have children with special needs, and you have little or no other option but to provide them with constant physical support. When the amount of physical contact you provide is directly related to your child's health and quality of life, being "touched out" may be your default setting, stretching you to the breaking point.

WHERE DOES MY HELP COME FROM?

Feeling overwhelmed by touch brings into focus two realities—our human limitations and our sin nature. We are fallen and deteriorating creatures. As a result of Adam's sin in the garden of Eden, death has spread to all people (Romans 5:12). Our bodies grow weary, and therefore, our children's unrelenting touch can drain our stamina. And when we're drained, it's all too easy to sin against our children by responding to their touch with resentment or even anger.

When we feel "touched out" by our children, we can draw strength from almighty God. If we want to be fruitful in discipling our children and pour out good things into them, then we must first be filled up with the truth of God's Word ourselves. Similarly, we must seek God's sustaining strength to love children sacrificially with our very bodies.

We must seek God's sustaining strength to love children sacrificially with our very bodies.

Too often, however, we are like the Samaritan woman whom Jesus speaks to in John 4:1–15. The woman in this passage comes to draw water from a well to quench her physical thirst and has an unexpected encounter with Jesus. He draws the woman's attention to her deeper spiritual thirst, inviting her to ask Him for living water that will never leave her thirsty. As parents, we desperately need the living water available in Jesus, but we often look only to physical solutions, especially when our physical body is in distress.

While conventional wisdom tells us self-care is the answer, we must remember that our true and lasting help comes from the Lord (Psalm 121:2). We ultimately won't find the respite we so desperately need in spa days, new exercise routines, or date nights away from our kids. While these are all good things that can indeed provide temporary relief, they won't provide the supernatural, soul-level restoration we need when children deplete us.

It is the Lord who restores our souls (Psalm 23:3, NKJV) and clothes us with strength (Psalm 18:32), enabling us to face our daily challenges — including meeting our children's need for touch. When children are pushing us to our physical limits, breaking past our boundaries to cut even into our sleep, we must seek the One who is boundless and has no need for slumber or sleep (Psalm 121:3–4).

JESUS AND TOUCH

When we're feeling touched out as parents, we might consider how Jesus used touch so powerfully in His earthly ministry. Moved with compassion, Jesus provided immediate healing to a leper who desperately begged Him for help (Mark 1:39–42). Jesus, who was perfectly able to heal people at a distance (Matthew 8:5–13, John 4:46–54), chose to reach out and *touch* the leper. In doing this, Jesus not only healed the man's physical wounds but also reached soul-deep into a heart undoubtedly wounded by the extreme social isolation resulting from having a contagious skin disease in the ancient world.

While Jesus worked in many ways, He had a tendency to minister through touch. In healing two blind men, and in healing a deaf man who had difficulty speaking, Jesus also used touch (Matthew 9:27–29, Mark 7:31–34). What compassion Jesus had to choose tactile healing with people who suffered from their other senses failing them!

And, parents, pay special attention to the way Jesus reached out to children in the Scriptures. In a wonderful display of fatherly love, Jesus actually scooped up babies and children in His arms, laid His hands on them, and blessed them (Mark 10:13–16, Luke 18:15–17). When His disciples tried to shoo the kids away, He rebuked the disciples, encouraged the children to come to Him—and even commanded His disciples to be more like the children in their wide-eyed welcome of the kingdom of God.

WITHDRAWING TO THE FATHER

Jesus often weathered great intensity of touch. In Luke 8:40–48, the crowd following Jesus was practically crushing Him. A woman in that crowd reached for Him, desperate for healing, and Jesus sensed that power had gone out of Him to meet the woman's need. While we are certainly not Jesus, we might feel at times that "power" has gone out of us—in a different and depleting way—from our children's constant touch!

When we feel this way, we can look again to Jesus's example and consider His ways. While Jesus's ministry was public, He regularly prayed in private (Luke 9:18, Mark 1:35). In fact, He "often withdrew to deserted places and prayed" (Luke 5:16). Despite the unrelenting demands of massive crowds and their many desperate needs, Jesus had a practice of slipping away by Himself to pray and seek the face of His Father.

Jesus often weathered great intensity of touch.

HOPE FOR TOUCHED-OUT PARENTS

If you find yourself touched out, ask God for strength in your weakness so that you can love your children sacrificially, especially when their needs take a toll on your body. You can also ask God for wisdom and patience in training your children to respect healthy boundaries around your needs to sleep or work uninterrupted—or simply have time alone to recharge.

Consider how you might imitate the ways of Jesus—how He reached out and touched those who needed Him, how He gathered children into His arms and blessed them, and how He regularly took time away to pray and be refreshed in the presence of His Father. And every time your child clings to you, let it be a tangible reminder to cling to God with the same deep trust and dependence, knowing He listens and attends to millions of prayers and needs but never grows weak, weary, or overwhelmed.

This essay was originally published in issue 8 of Gospel at Home™ *magazine.*

Consider how Jesus used touch
so powerfully in His earthly ministry.

Growing in Grace
in Motherhood

Our Sinfulness and God's Good Work

HELEN HUMMEL

One hot Tennessee evening several summers back—as the crickets and the frogs sang in the darkness outside—I sat inside a friend's living room with several other women from church. We were discussing a book our group had been reading that summer when the conversation turned to the topic of motherhood. As one of the only women in the group without children at the time, I was tempted to tune out, assuming I wouldn't be able to relate to the talk of toddler temper tantrums and fourth-grade field trips. But then, someone said something that completely captured my attention.

One woman, recounting the challenges of raising small children, began to talk about the unique way that parenting often reveals her own sinfulness—her shortcomings and struggles, her failures and mistakes.

Around the circle, woman after woman chimed in, each sharing her own stories of motherhood. And even though I didn't yet have children of my own, I quickly realized I could relate to each of these women and the stories they shared.

In my closest relationships with others—marriage, family, friendships—I often see my own sin on display. And I wonder if the same is true for you. Somehow, it is often our most intimate relationships that expose our sinful human nature. And while it can be discouraging to see this displayed with those we love most, what if these moments are actually a gift of grace? What if God is actually using these moments for good?

A GIFT OF GRACE

What are the relationships that most often expose your own sinfulness? Is it your relationship with your spouse, your family of origin, or maybe even your own children?

While getting married to my husband was one of the sweetest experiences of my life, it was also a bit sobering, as all of a sudden it exposed my sinful nature in ways I didn't expect. In the early months of marriage, it felt like my sin was often lurking just around the corner—making its presence known in the frustrating moments when I was too quick to speak and too slow to listen, in the self-centered moments when I would put my own desires first, in the prideful moments when I was unwilling to admit I was wrong, and in so many moments in between.

I saw something similar unfold several years later, when we welcomed our first child—a precious baby girl—into the world. As I learned to be her mom, I quickly found myself falling short. I had imagined myself as the mom with limitless patience, love, and grace for myself and others. But between round-the-clock feedings, more diaper changes than I could've possibly imagined, and what seemed like endless cycles of crying, I quickly felt my resolve crumble. More often than I'd care to admit, I reverted to selfishness, irritation, and bitterness instead of patience, love, and grace.

By God's grace, I have grown in some ways since then. But in many areas, I continue to wrestle with similar experiences—experiences that feel like a road sign pointing directly to my own fallenness. And, as someone who has been a believer for many years now, these moments can feel quite discouraging—especially when it seems like I deal with the same sins over and over again. If I'm not careful, I can catch myself wondering, *Shouldn't I have this all sorted out by now?*

While we should indeed lament our sin, what if there is a different way to look at these painful moments? As discouraging as they may feel at the time, what if they are actually a unique opportunity for us to see our need for a Savior more clearly?

Now, of course, God does not desire sin for us; after all, He clearly instructs His people: "Be holy as I am holy" (Leviticus 11:44–45, 19:2, 20:7; 1 Peter 1:16). But God does promise to use all things for our good and His glory—even the hard things (Romans 8:28). What if God wants to use these painful moments to expose not only our sinfulness but also how much we need Him? What if these very moments can actually propel us to rely on Jesus more and more as we slowly but surely grow in sanctification?

WHAT TO DO WHEN CONFRONTED WITH YOUR OWN SIN

So, what are we to do in the moments in our relationships—with our spouses, kids, friends, coworkers, or fellow church members—when our own sin becomes painfully evident? Here are four steps that may be helpful.

1. *Confess.*

   The moments that expose our own sinfulness can often make us want to run and hide. We rarely want to address our own sin, and this can sometimes lead us to ignore it or downplay it. Proverbs 28:13 speaks to this desire when it says, "The one who conceals his sins will not prosper, but whoever confesses and renounces them will find mercy." Similarly, James 5:16 instructs us to confess our sins to one another, and 1 John 1:9 reminds us that God is "faithful and righteous to forgive us our sins and to cleanse us from all unrighteousness." When confronted with our own sin, we first must acknowledge it—to ourselves, to our God, and to others.

2. *Repent.*

   Closely related to the idea of confession is the idea of repentance. When we repent, we acknowledge our wrongdoing. But repentance does not only involve admitting our sin; it also involves turning away from our sin and turning toward Christ. We depend on Him as we desire to walk away from sin and into obedience. And as we do so, we keep our eyes on Jesus, the "pioneer and perfecter of our faith," knowing He will help us run with endurance the race set before us (Hebrews 12:1–2).

3. *Thank God.*

   As uncomfortable as it can be to be confronted with our own sinfulness, especially in our relationships with other people, we can view these moments as gifts of grace from our good God. While Christ makes us new creations at the moment of salvation (2 Corinthians 5:17), the work of sanctification is ongoing, and it isn't always easy. Even in the moments we fail, we can thank God for the ways He continues to work in our lives through all circumstances. He has promised that He will work everything together for good (Romans 8:28), and this includes the difficult moments of our sanctification.

4. Trust God.

In Paul's letter to the Philippians, he calls each of us to work out our own salvation with fear and trembling (Philippians 2:12). But, in the very next verse, Paul reminds us that this is not something we do alone. He writes, "For it is God who is working in you both to will and to work according to his good purpose" (Philippians 2:13). In the moments when we are confronted with our own sinfulness, we can take comfort in the fact that God is still working in us. The process of sanctification is lifelong, and it is initiated by God Himself, who will always be faithful to finish the good work He starts (Philippians 1:6).

REMEMBER GOD'S FAITHFULNESS

So, the next time you are confronted with your own sinfulness, remember that God is continuing His good work in you. Don't hide from your sinfulness, but instead, commit to the hard but holy work of confession, repentance, and turning to Him as you live in relationship with others in this broken world. And thank God for the opportunities He gives you to rely on Him as He conforms you more to the image of His beloved Son (Romans 8:29).

If you are in Christ, you can take comfort in the glorious truth that Jesus has already justified you, making you right in the eyes of the Father. And Jesus will be faithful to finish His work, bringing you to glorification one day, too (Romans 8:30).

This essay was originally published in January 2023 on The Daily Grace® Blog.

Thank God for the opportunities
He gives you to rely on Him.

How to Stop Losing It with Your Kids

KRISTYN PEREZ

W e've all been there. It's been a long day, and your child JUST. WON'T. OBEY. You feel your blood start to boil. Doesn't your child know how hard you've worked for him this week, how much you sacrificed for him? Yet his room is a mess, he is complaining about what he doesn't have, and he just won't obey.

You lose it. You explode on your child in an outburst of anger, feeling simultaneously justified for your anger and guilty for your lack of self-control.

Surely there has to be a better way. While one article could never solve all of our parenting problems, here are a few ideas for how to stop losing it with our kids. If you are wanting to know how to change your parenting patterns, consider the following:

PRAY

We can do nothing without God's help (John 15:5). If you find that you keep yelling at your children, ask the Lord for help. He wants us to be good parents who love our children well. He gives us all we need for life and godliness (2 Peter 1:3). Ask that He would grow your patience, compassion, and self-control. Ask for wisdom on how to discipline your children.

And not only this, but ask that the Lord would change your children. As parents, we are called to lovingly discipline our children (Proverbs 3:11–12), yet sometimes we think it's all up to us. We forget that God is powerful, and He can change hearts. Ask God to help your child grow in the areas that you've noticed are lacking.

SEEK GODLY MENTORS AND FRIENDS

Especially if your upbringing has left much to be desired, seek godly mentors to disciple you in your parenting. An older woman in your local church can help you work through the specific details of your parenting. She can offer practical wisdom on how to shepherd your child with grace and truth. Books such as *Shepherding a Child's Heart* by Tedd Tripp can also help provide biblical parenting wisdom. It is also helpful to find a trusted friend and confess your sins of impatience, anger, or fear. Seek accountability with friends about how you react to your children in stressful moments of the day. Ask a friend to help you think through healthy parenting patterns and evaluate methods to manage the stressful moments in your parenting day.

LOOK FOR IDOLS IN YOUR HEART

In Scripture, children are called to obey their parents (Ephesians 6:1). It is part of our role as parents to lovingly discipline our children and teach them to obey, in part, so that they can learn how to obey the Lord. But when we react with impulsive anger at our kid's disobedience, these moments often reveal something deeper in our hearts. Often, we are less concerned that our kids disobeyed God's law. We're mad that our kids disobeyed our law and disrupted the reigning idols of our hearts.

Consider for a moment: When you yell at your child, why do you yell? When you lose it on your children, what are you craving? In the heat of the moment, are you primarily concerned because your child isn't obeying the Lord or because your child isn't obeying you? Are you wanting respect, quiet, or a clean house? Are you just wanting a break? All of these are good things, but when they become the ultimate things we seek, they become idols in our lives that are being threatened by our children. We will sin to get them or sin when we don't get them.

If you are having trouble identifying your motives, consider your patterns of anger. For example, do you typically lose it on your child when he misbehaves in front of others, and you feel embarrassed? Or, is it primarily when your authority feels threatened through disobedience? Is it when the house is dirty or when the kids are loud? Our impatience in these moments often reveals sin within our hearts when our kingdom is being threatened.

To be clear, identifying our motives does not mean that we do not discipline our children. Rather, it gives us the time and space to shepherd our children with the right motives in mind—primarily for God's glory and the good of our children.

MEDITATE ON GOD'S MERCY IN PARENTING

God is the perfect Father (Matthew 5:48). He is quick to forgive (1 John 1:9). He does not explode with anger when we make a mistake (Psalm 103:8). He is long-suffering, patient, and kind (2 Peter 3:9, Ephesians 2:6–7). He does not ignore right and wrong. God perfectly disciplines His children, and He does so out of love. Truly, God is the perfect parent—but we are not.

When we fail (and we will), we can model humble repentance before our children. We can apologize for our lack of patience or sinful anger and ask for their forgiveness. We can point to God's grace and remember that our role as a parent is not to be perfect but to point our kids to the perfect Savior. He equips us and sanctifies us as we parent. He will help us grow in patience, wisdom, and love. God's mercies are new every morning (Lamentations 3:22–23), and He gives strength for today.

Our role as a parent is not to be perfect but to point our kids to the perfect Savior.

This essay was originally published in May 2022 on The Daily Grace® Blog.

I Keep Messing Up:
Will God Still Love Me?

SHELBY TURNER

I sigh and let my head fall into my hands. I've done it—again. I've let the frustrations of the day and the stress of the moment push me over the edge. I gave vent to my anger, and the undeserved recipients of it are, once more, my children. As my white-hot temper cools, I feel other emotions rising up in me.

I'm disappointed that my immaturity is showing. I'm embarrassed that I don't have this problem under control yet. I'm saddened by the pain I've caused to those around me. I'm desperate to make better choices. I'm hopeless that I could ever change.

At that moment, I usually feel like I am the only one who can't seem to overcome my vices. But, in reality, I know that every believer struggles with sin. I've sat in vulnerable circles with friends who dared to share their inner battles enough times to know that we all struggle. Whether it is jealousy, lust, pride, faithlessness, bitterness, or anything else—everyone wrestles with sin. And almost all of us wonder about these close-clinging sins that beg for an answer: *I keep messing up. Will God really keep forgiving me?*

I want to assure you that for all of those in Christ, the answer to this question is a resounding "Yes!" Yes, God will forgive all of your sins. Even the ones that have plagued you the longest and consumed you the most. God's forgiveness does not depend in the slightest degree on what you do or don't do. It depends wholly, completely, and to the fullest degree on Jesus Christ.

Romans 5:18–21 gives us all the reassurance we need to believe that all sins are forgiven in Christ. This passage is included at the end of this reflection for you to slowly read and contemplate. But, if we were to sum it up, it would say:

Your sin condemns you, but God declares you justified in Christ.

Your disobedience labels you as a sinner, but through
Christ's obedience, you are labeled righteous.

Where your sin multiplies, God's grace multiplies even more.

Sin once reigned in you, but through Jesus, grace now reigns.

Jesus's sacrifice is enough. At every moment of your life, whether you are at your best or your very worst, the grace of God covers all your mistakes. It is not logical. You will not make sense of it. Grace covers, in great excess, all the sins of those who have found salvation in Christ. What an overwhelmingly beautiful truth for all of us who struggle with sin. So, what do we do in response to God's grace? For it is one thing to understand this truth and another thing to believe it and live according to it.

According to Scripture, we should confess our sins in response to God's grace. First John 1:9 explains this as it says, "If we confess our sins, he is faithful and righteous to forgive us our sins and to cleanse us from all unrighteousness." Confessing your sins can sound like this: "Lord, I've messed up again. Please, forgive me for..." This is something we should pray daily. But we should also remember that God's grace extends beyond forgiveness. In His grace, He also teaches us how to deny godlessness and live in a godly way (Titus 2:11–12). I've heard it said that God's grace is a grace that doesn't leave us where we are, but it calls us up to maturity. We should pursue the path to maturity that grace lays out for us. That path is long. The travel along it is often slow. There are setbacks. We will need camaraderie and accountability. It requires prayer and the transforming of our minds through Scripture. But, on that path, we are never alone. And the steps we take on it do not affect our standing before God. Our standing with God does not depend on what we do. It depends only on what Jesus has done.

In Christ, all of our sins are forgiven. God gives great grace to every sinner who repents. It is grace that abounds; grace that cannot be outmatched or outrun; grace that Jesus freely gives. When we wonder, *Can He really forgive me still?*, we can choose to let grace and not sin reign in our hearts, minds, and thoughts. God says that grace reigns. Praise God! May we receive and respond to it like the outrageous gift it is.

So then, as through one trespass there is condemnation for everyone, so also through one righteous act there is justification leading to life for everyone. For just as through one man's disobedience the many were made sinners, so also through the one man's obedience the many will be made righteous. The law came along to multiply the trespass. But where sin multiplied, grace multiplied even more so that, just as sin reigned in death, so also grace will reign through righteousness, resulting in eternal life through Jesus Christ our Lord.

ROMANS 5:18–21

This essay was originally published in March 2022 on The Daily Grace® Blog.

We should confess our sins
in response to God's grace.

Handling Stress: Exploding, Imploding, or Peace

KRISTYN PEREZ

Recently, I've been having lots of conversations about stress. These days, it feels like the whole world is under stress. Some are stressed because of politics and pandemics. Others feel stress due to loss, marital conflict, or unemployment.

And what about you? Are you under stress today? Have you found yourself snapping quickly, crying more easily, and trying to escape your negative emotions? Do you feel excessive tension in your neck and back, even right now? Do you find yourself yelling at your children, your husband, or your friends over seemingly minor conflicts? Do you feel burnt out at your job? Do you want relief in your relationships — to somehow escape from this "new normal"? Do you feel a pressure rising within you, like a sizzling, steaming Crock-Pot® ready to explode?

And what should we do when we're stressed anyway? Should we cancel our plans and open that pint of ice cream? Do we turn on the TV and numb out the world? Society encourages self-care or cutting out the toxic people in our lives. The outbreak of the pandemic — and its long-term implications — threw a kink into some of our normal go-to's. Suddenly, we discovered it was much more difficult to deal with our stress by having our nails done, getting massages, or going to the movies. And we quickly learned we couldn't escape the people we live with, especially if we're all working or doing school from home together. How can we relieve our stress when this is our reality?

In light of this conversation about stress, the following words from Paul are remarkable. Paul was no stranger to stress. His physical body was strained by multiple shipwrecks and beatings, as well as a stoning (2 Corinthians 11:25). He experienced betrayal, mocking, slander, and false accusations. Yet, to the very people who betrayed him in the past, he says:

> *Now we have this treasure in clay jars, so that this extraordinary power may be from God and not from us. We are afflicted in every way but not crushed; we are perplexed but not in despair; we are persecuted but not abandoned; we are struck down but not destroyed. We always carry the death of Jesus in our body, so that the life of Jesus may also be displayed in our body. For we who live are always being given over to death for Jesus's sake, so that Jesus's life may also be displayed in our mortal flesh.* (2 Corinthians 4:7–11)

In this life, we will be afflicted, perplexed, persecuted, and struck down. We may experience a season of extraordinary grief or a time of tremendous sacrifice for the sake of another. We may even take up our cross and follow Jesus yet still wonder where He is and why this is all so hard.

Faithfulness is not the absence of trouble; it is clinging to God through that trouble. For, as Paul says, even when we experience pressure from all sides, afflicted in every way, we are never alone. Even in burnout, betrayal, and exhaustion, we are never forsaken. Christ, the suffering servant, knows our pain intimately and carries our burdens. He took on the weight of our sins, every single one of them, and died for them. And not only this, but He rose from the grave, and He promises us new, eternal, and abundant life with Him.

Christ, who suffered more than we ever could, knows our troubles. He is with us through them. During His life on earth, Jesus experienced pressure, affliction, and betrayal. In His stress, He turned to the Father, pouring out tears like blood. For indeed, faithfulness is not an absence of trouble but an active dependence on the Father in the midst of it.

So, in light of this, we pray. Daily, we continually—unceasingly—pour out our hearts to God. We tell Him everything in prayer, opening up the steamer on the proverbial Crock-Pot® and asking for His help.

We maintain the common graces of calendar planning, exercise, healthy eating, church community, and thankfulness. And we press in to remember—remembering that we're not alone, remembering what Christ has done, remembering that God knows our pain and that He carries us.

In our suffering, we have the opportunity to point to the sufficiency of Christ. Even when everything within us tells us to protect ourselves and flee, we can remain steadfast, proclaiming that *Christ is enough, and He is coming again! This is not the end of my story!* When in hope we identify with Christ's suffering, we display His power that is so mightily at work within us. God has chosen to give us these weak and limited bodies so that we can show God's power through our weaknesses. Each of us has limited time, resources, energy, and opportunities, and whenever these are threatened or stretched beyond our limits, we will feel pressure. But as Hudson Taylor says, "It doesn't matter, really, how great the pressure is…it only matters where the pressure lies. See that it never comes between you and the Lord—then, the greater the pressure, the more it presses you to His breast."[4]

In our stress and tension of the season, let us press nearer into the loving arms of our Savior. He offers to carry our burdens and give us rest (Matthew 11:28–30). He offers a supernatural peace—one that surpasses understanding (Philippians 4:7). He reminds us that even youths become weary, and young men fall, but those who trust the Lord will renew their strength (Isaiah 40:30–31). We can cast all our cares on Him because He cares for us (1 Peter 5:7).

---

*Faithfulness is not the absence of trouble;
it is clinging to God through that trouble.*

This essay was originally published in issue 27 of Be Still Magazine®.

Interrupted by God

KRISTYN PEREZ

Sickness has found its way into my household. My young kids who struggle to share their toys seem glad to share their germs—cycling colds, eye infections, and tummy aches throughout our family for weeks on end. Although these seasons can be invitations to slow down and rest, they can also be discouraging when there is seemingly no end in sight. As I've slowed down the past month, I've been asking the question, "Lord, what are You trying to teach me?"

Have you ever had seasons like this—days filled with unexpected interruptions that make you slow down, change course, or reflect on life? When your plans are interrupted by illness, job loss, or conflict, how do you respond?

To me, these interruptions often feel bothersome. "My plans" are in disarray. My control is gone. My days feel ruined. I get uncomfortable as I discover that my true desires for the days are exposed. My faith, or lack thereof, is revealed. But what if these interruptions weren't really interruptions at all? What if they were invitations to join God in His plans?

So often as Americans, we want our lives to go smoothly. We want healthy bodies, financial abundance, and as little inconveniences as possible. Unfortunately, if this is our hope, we will be disappointed. The God of the Bible does not promise these things this side of heaven. Instead, He invites us into His mission to bring healing and hope to a broken world. He offers us a chance to know Him and to get our hands dirty as we love God and neighbor.

But this desire for ease isn't just an American problem. In one of His parables, Jesus tells the story of a man who was attacked by robbers on the road to Jericho. The robbers not only took the man's clothes, but also beat him, leaving him for dead. In God's providence, several other men also traveled on the road that day. The first of these was a priest, a godly man who knew the law. He knew God's words and could have recited them from memory. At this moment, though, he conveniently forgot the Scripture's teachings to love his neighbor and take care of the vulnerable. Instead, when he saw the bleeding man, he kept walking. A Levite also passed by, leaving him for dead.

Maybe these men were afraid for their own safety. Maybe they didn't want to dirty themselves according to Jewish customs, or maybe they were so set on their plans that they could not be interrupted. Either way, they continued on with their days as scheduled.

Finally, a Samaritan passed by. It would have been unthinkable that a Samaritan would help a Jew. Yet seeing the bloody man, the foreigner bandaged his wounds and brought him to safety. Not only did the Samaritan risk his life to do so, but he also provided for the man's financial needs. He left the injured man with an innkeeper, promising to pay for his expenses when he returned. Jesus concluded the story by asking, "Which of these three, do you think, proved to be a neighbor to the man who fell among the robbers? . . . You go, and do likewise'" (Luke 10:25–37, ESV).

I've read this story a thousand times, but what stood out to me in this season is the fact that all three men in this story were going somewhere. They were all "busy men" who had plans for the day. And yet, only one allowed his plans to be interrupted by God. Only one engaged with the brokenness of another when given the chance. The others turned blind eyes, too afraid or busy to help.

On these verses, Dietrich Bonhoeffer says:

We must be ready to allow ourselves to be interrupted by God. God will be constantly crossing our paths and canceling our plans by sending us people with claims and petitions. We may pass them by, preoccupied with our more important tasks as the priest passed by the man who had fallen among thieves, perhaps—reading the Bible...It is a strange fact that Christians and even ministers frequently consider their work so important and urgent that they will allow nothing to disturb them. They think they are doing God a service in this, but actually they are disdaining God's "crooked yet straight path." They do not want a life that is crossed and balked. But it is part of the discipline of humility that we must not spare our hand where it can perform a service and that we do not assume that our schedule is our own to manage, but allow it to be arranged by God.[5]

So, I've been asking myself this season, *And here, in life's little interruptions, God is refining me. Will I let God interrupt my days, or will I turn a blind eye to those whom God would have me love?* Just as God was sovereign in the story of the Good Samaritan, God knows my story from the beginning. He knew that my family would pass eye infections to one another seven different times. He knew that it would tire me to wash three sets of sheets every day for a month. He crafted the days so that I would have to cancel play-dates and stay home for more days than I'd like. He knew it all from the beginning of time, and in His sovereignty, He allowed these little sicknesses to pass within our family time and time again.

And here, in life's little interruptions, God is refining me. He's showing me to trust Him in the mundane, to bring order and healing within my own home to my little neighbors. He's teaching me how to love little ones who can't yet take care of themselves. He's showing me what it means to be faithful in the day-to-day interruptions of life.

This year, I've been praying for God to grow my faith. I've wanted this to happen through big, miraculous moments, but what if God is growing my faith through the normal, day-to-day moments?

What I have viewed as interruptions of greater things, are actually His invitations to press into Him in faith. After all, though my plans may be interrupted, His plans never are.

This essay was originally published in issue 17 of Be Still Magazine®.

And here, in life's little interruptions,
God is refining me.

The Joy of Interruptions: Reflecting on God's Character When Our Plans Change

KRYSTAL DICKSON

Though I am a creature of habit, I am not a morning person by nature. But over the years of sleepless nights with young children, I have actually come to appreciate the early hours of the day. On one particular morning, I tiptoed down the stairs to grab a cup of coffee and start my day before the sunrise. But as soon as I sat down with my Bible and took my first sip of hot coffee, I heard the creaking of a bedroom door, followed by the excited pitter-patter of tiny feet that got louder and louder until I saw a messy-haired, half-asleep child standing before me. As he climbed into my lap, snuggling up next to me while sitting on my Bible and nearly knocking over my coffee, I experienced a flood of emotions—thankfulness for my child, frustration over my interrupted morning, anxiety over my to-do list. I sighed and thought to myself, *I'll try again tomorrow.*

We all have examples of when our plans go awry. It could be a small inconvenience in your day, like a child waking up early. Or it could be a fork in the road that changes the course of your life, like an unexpected diagnosis. Our days are often filled with interruptions, big and small, to our normal rhythms. Without reflecting on who God is, even the smallest obstacles can feel impossible to overcome. What we believe about God will inform how we respond when things don't go our way. Let's consider a couple of things that are important to remember about God when things don't go our way.

GOD ACTS WITH PURPOSE (ROMANS 8:28–30, EPHESIANS 1:11)

God works in our lives with great purpose and intentionality. Nothing is by chance or accident. When we pray about circumstances in our lives, we ask God to answer our prayers according to His will—and rightly so. There are verses that speak directly to God's will, and interestingly, these verses often center around our sanctification through how we respond to our circumstances (1 Thessalonians 4:3–5, 5:16–18). A change in plans allows us the opportunity to walk in His ways and not our own. In His wisdom, God chooses to refine us and sanctify us through our circumstances.

GOD IS SOVEREIGN (LAMENTATIONS 3:37–39)

Ultimately, we can choose to submit our lives and plans to God because He is sovereign. The God of the universe is sovereign over traffic, nap times, overdue work deadlines, everything. He is over every minute and every hour of our days. Do we find comfort in that reality, or are we tempted to push against it? Do we find rest in the sovereignty of God, or do we try to take control of the situation? When we remember that we are not in control, we can truly rest in God regardless of our circumstances.

When our days do not go according to plan, we can respond in a variety of ways. Idols of comfort and control can rise to the surface, demanding our allegiance. Our response to change will reveal who or what sits on the throne of our heart. We may be tempted to avoid God or try to be our own god, forcing circumstances to bend to our will rather than God's. Instead, let the discomfort of change draw us into deeper intimacy with the Lord. Rejoice in the God of our salvation, the One who never changes!

This essay was originally published in January 2022 on The Daily Grace® Blog.

Finding Relief from the Pressure to Do It All

KRYSTAL DICKSON

What defines a good day for you? Think about how you respond when someone asks you that question. When my husband comes home from work, he always asks me how my day was. My response defines a "good day" as one that was productive: "I got so much done. It was great!" Yet more times than not, I will respond with something like, "It was a hard day. I barely got anything done."

To some degree, we will feel the pressure to "do it all." Unfortunately, that pressure can overshadow our joy, turning minor moments into defining markers of our day. There never seems to be enough time to accomplish everything we want to do. And even on the days when every box is checked off, there can be the temptation to add "just one more thing" to the list, cramming tasks into the margins of our lives. We can crown productivity as our ultimate aim in life—but at what cost?

In our fast-paced world that screams "more is more," is it possible to find relief from the pressure to do it all?

LIMITS ARE A GIFT.

God created us beautifully and intentionally. He gave us our senses so that we could experience the world around us. He fashioned us with talents, abilities, and passions. And God also made our bodies to need rest and sustenance. He did not create us to stay awake for days on end or to go without food or water. As independent and self-sufficient as we try to be, at some point, our bodies will clue us in that we are not limitless. We feel aches and pains. We grow tired. We need relief. But when we live within our limits, we honor God in the way He has made us. Our limits are a gift.

Even in our limited nature, God has entrusted us with work to do. We see this even as we look back to the early moments of creation when God gave Adam and Eve the work of dominion (Genesis 1:26–28). As women today, work comes in a variety of packages and is rarely neatly tied with a bow. The work of motherhood can spill over into our vocational work or even replace it. We care for a variety of people before we care for ourselves. Though we may love the roles God has given us and the work He has called us to, it can be tiring trying to keep up with it all. Work and stewardship are good things with which we can honor the Lord. Yet we do this within the limits He has also given to each of us.

Seeing our limits as a gift and operating within our God-given boundaries means saying "no" sometimes. It means being humble enough to recognize when taking on an exciting opportunity would be unwise, given your capacity and ability. It means being okay with things undone.

This does not mean we throw every responsibility out the window in the name of rest. But it does mean recognizing what God is actually calling us to do. We do not need to meet every need. We just need to be faithful to what God has entrusted to each of us. We all have important work to do. And we all have limits. Both of these things are true and good as they come from the loving hands of our heavenly Father.

WE SERVE A GOD WHO IS LIMITLESS.

When we give in to the overwhelming pressure of perfect productivity, we neglect to remember the character of God. He is infinite, sovereign, and all-knowing. He is limitless. Giving in to the pressure to do it all often means we try to step into God's role. We want to be infinite. We want to be sovereign. We want to be all-knowing. We want to fix and make and provide and sustain. We want to be limitless.

No wonder we are so tired.

Exhaustion and burnout can happen when we neglect to see ourselves and our God rightly. Just like when we try to go without sleep, we stretch beyond our limits by taking on attributes of God that we were not designed to embody. Remembering the nature of our great God should humble us as we reassume our roles as dependent creatures in need of His mercy.

OUR LIMITS DRAW US TO THE ONE WHO PROVIDES TRUE REST.

Second Corinthians 12:9 reminds us that God's grace is sufficient for us, for His power is made perfect in our weakness. There is grace for us when we have our completed to-do list, but there is also grace for us when not a single box is checked off. Our worth is not found in checked-off to-do lists but is found in Christ alone. Jesus came to free us from the shackles of our self-sufficiency. When we rest in Him alone, we have all that we need. By His Spirit, we can pursue wisdom in the decisions we make, and when we do, we can trust the Lord with the outcome.

The next time you are asked about your day, consider your response. How do you define what is good? Is it through what you have accomplished? Or is it resting in the finished work of Christ? Starting from a place of rest in the Lord will ensure that our priorities are straight. We think we will find relief when we finally do it all. But then that to-do list grows longer each day, making relief seem elusive and unattainable. Yet the relief comes when we realize that we do not have to do it all—in fact, we are completely and utterly unable to do so. We can work joyfully unto the Lord, thankful that we do not uphold the world but that we worship the God who does (Colossians 1:17, Hebrews 1:3).

Jesus came to free us from the shackles
of our self-sufficiency.

This essay was originally published in issue 31 of Be Still Magazine®.

How Accepting Our Limits in Motherhood Enables Us to Be Generous

TIFFANY DICKERSON

We live in a time when the world tells moms that they can "do it all." This means being expected to act as a full-time wife, church volunteer, employee, friend, coach, cheerleader, caregiver, laundromat, chef, maid, cab driver, teacher, gym member, dog walker, and more. Indeed, moms embody some version of these roles on a daily basis. And at the end of the day, we fall into bed exhausted, mentally going through our long list for the next day before we drift off to sleep.

I'm sure many of you reading this have thought of several roles you could add to the list above. Though our world would love for us to think we truly can do it all, our exhaustion and hope for a vacation tell a different story. There is always give and take in our lives. It is a continual reminder that we are finite beings. For followers of Christ, however, this shouldn't cause us to despair. Instead, we lean into the life-giving generosity of our great God as He enables us to fulfill the roles He's called us to—in His strength and not our own.

Overarchingly, moms are generous people. The number of hats we wear serves as evidence that we are willing to give up personal time, space, and rest in order to make sure our families are happy, healthy, full, on time, and well-rested. We are generous with our very lives because we love the people God has entrusted to us. And while admitting our finite natures might seem counterintuitive to generosity, we are actually more generous when we admit our limitations and entrust every aspect of our lives to our generous God. It is when we come to the end of ourselves that we remember how good God is and that it is our weakness that brings Him glory.

The Apostle Paul speaks about God's power in his own weakness when he shares the Lord's message in 2 Corinthians 12:9: "My grace is sufficient for you, for my power is perfected in weakness." When we lean into our weaknesses, accept that we are finite, and rest in the infinite generosity of the Lord, it is then that we bring Him glory. Rather than believing we can do it all, we admit that we cannot and find our strength in the Lord instead. Paul also declares this in the second part of 2 Corinthians 12:9, when he writes, "Therefore, I will most gladly boast all the more about my weaknesses, so that Christ's power may reside in me."

God's glory and generosity manifest themselves through His greatest gift—salvation through Jesus Christ. Christ defeated the weakness of humanity when He died on the cross and rose from the grave. Sin and death no longer have an eternal hold on our lives. But while we still live and breathe on this side of eternity, our earthly bodies face weakness—they are finite. Yet we serve an infinite God who has given us His Word, His Son, and His Spirit to help us grow in holiness and steward our lives for His glory.

Admitting we cannot "do it all" is the first step in leaning into our weakness, growing in generosity, and allowing the power of Christ to work through us. But how can we steward our lives generously while also accepting that we have limits? The best place to begin is by knowing the character of God. When we seek to know who God is, we quickly find that His generosity is limitless. Through every one of His attributes, He displays the love of a generous Father who never tires. When we rest in His unchanging nature, we shift our priorities and learn how to say "no," even to good things, and we do so for the betterment of our walk with Christ and for our families.

So often, we think that saying "yes" to everything is the most generous thing to do, but in reality, it spreads us so thin that we cannot give our best to any of our roles. Our default reactions and emotions tend to be frustration, exhaustion, resentment, or anger. In contrast, saying "no" and admitting that we cannot do everything allows us to display Christ's power within us. We focus on our most important roles and how we can bring glory to the Lord through them.

There are many roles as a mom that are non-negotiable, which makes discerning what to say "yes" and "no" to so important. However, the Lord can help! In James 1:5, Jesus's half-brother James says, "Now if any of you lacks wisdom, he should ask God—who gives to all generously and ungrudgingly—and it will be given to him." When we seek the Lord for wisdom and discernment, we can trust that He will give them to us. We can take our schedules and roles to Him in prayer and ask Him to help us know what to pour our time into and what to pause for a season or even permanently.

Below are some questions and thoughts to ponder as you diagnose your current limits. Take time to consider these questions in light of Colossians 3:17, which says, "And whatever you do, in word or in deed, do everything in the name of the Lord Jesus, giving thanks to God the Father through him." Live generously for Jesus by leaning into His power when you are weak and ask Him to help you discern how you can generously give your time to Him, your family, and the Church.

1. *What role(s) might you be saying "yes" to that takes away from your time with the Lord, your family, and your church community?*

2. *What might be your default emotions in your current roles? How can this help you diagnose when and how you need to scale back in order to be more generous?*

3. *What might you say "no" to for a season so that you can be more generous with your time in fewer roles?*

4. *When asked to take on a role, do not be afraid to ask for time to consider your response. Then, take time to pray, search the Word, and discuss it with your spouse or a trusted friend.*

This essay was originally published in issue 8 of Gospel at Home™ *magazine.*

Live generously for Jesus
by leaning into His power
when you are weak.

The Gospel Cure for Maternal Anxiety

GLORIA FURMAN

INFECTED WITH ANXIETY

Our pediatrician blesses my kids with decades of experience and friendly, grandfatherly care. When the kids sneeze in his presence, he says with flourishing gestures in several languages, "God bless you!" All of a sudden seeing the doctor isn't so scary.

Wise doctors know that part of the job also includes counseling parents. On one particular visit, I asked the doctor about the kind of day he was having. His brow furrowed as he answered thoughtfully, "The most infectious disease I treated was maternal anxiety."

SYMPTOMS AND DIAGNOSIS

The doctor's comment was a good reminder to me that it's worth getting a check-up on my own maternal anxiety. It seems like everywhere a mom turns these days there is some piece of information—article, conversation, book, commercial—that is designed to incite fear in her heart. Some nightmare or daymare that makes her heart pound. Some incident to make her nurturing instinct go into anxiety overdrive. Raising children in this fallen world can make a mom want to wrap her kids in bubblewrap and never leave the house!

In a lot of ways, anxiety does behave like a disease. Where the truth is suppressed and you're lacking spiritual nourishment, the conditions are ripe for anxiety to wreak havoc in your heart. Sometimes all it takes is glancing at a newspaper headline for anxiety to drive your heart to the edge of the cliffs of insanity and incite you to take a leap of unbelief without looking back. A friend confessed to me that one night she was so worried about her baby's

We must preach the gospel to ourselves day in and day out.

teething pain that her anxious thoughts multiplied in her heart until she laid awake for hours after the child had drifted off to sleep, horrified by the thought that one day she may have to attend her child's funeral. It might sound extreme, but we can all relate to the struggle to hold on to hope in the darkness.

Maternal anxiety is no laughing matter. Every mom knows that our world is rife with danger, evil, and death. Even our nonbelieving friends know this. So we scan the shelf of options for an antidote. Personally, when I'm hit with a case of maternal anxiety, I'm tempted to dull my anxious thoughts with distraction. If I am busy with other good things, then perhaps that looming challenge will just go away and I won't have to worry about it. When another friend is anxious, she wants to go on a quest for omniscience to control the outcome through research. If she just knows enough about the circumstances and solutions, then perhaps she won't have to worry about it. Other remedies like eating, spending money, and giving in to bitterness promise us an easy fix. If we can dull our senses, buy some more stuff, or vent our anger, perhaps we won't have to worry about it.

The barrage of anxiety-inducing situations and thoughts is unremitting. Dangerous fearmongering builds up like plaque in an artery, further restricting the circulation of life-giving truth. Anxious thoughts multiply like bacteria in a petri dish.

What's a mother to do? Back and forth we go — "positive thinking" meets horrible, fallen world, and back again. Is there any end to this rocking chair of anxiety?

BEWARE THE ANTI-GOSPEL

"Worrying is just part of being a mom" is not a cute job description to stencil over your kitchen doorway. It is an anti-gospel. And we must preach the gospel to ourselves day in and day out to combat that lie. We have to get off of the maternal anxiety rocking chair. We do not belong there. We must fight to remember that Christ died and rose again so that the worst thing imaginable—eternal separation from God—would never be reality for those whose hope is in Him.

When we remember that we have been rescued from a fate worse than death and we are always running headlong into future grace, our maternal anxiety gets put in its place. Even though situations arise where anxiety seems like the only available option because you can't understand what God is doing, by faith you can believe that He is always acting in accordance with His redeeming love. The worries that lurch your heart back and forth like a rocking chair lose their momentum in the face of this wondrous truth. In Christ, a mother's heart can rest. "In peace I will both lie down and sleep; for you alone, O LORD, make me dwell in safety" (Psalm 4:8, ESV).

HERD IMMUNITY FOR MATERNAL ANXIETY

Anxiety can go viral in a community, but so can gospel-saturated hope. We have to remember this for ourselves and for our sisters in Christ when they are struggling. Christ is exalted as moms point other moms to the gospel. As moms, we can remind each other of the hope we have in Christ, and we can use the gifts God has given us to build up the body of Christ. We can hold out God's Word to our sisters who are weakened by anxiety and anemic for the truth of God's Word.

I've been the beneficiary of this kind of nurturing. This morning a friend asked me over the phone, "How is your heart?" When I rehearsed my To-Worry-About List and concluded with the finale, "And I just don't see how this week is going to come together," she paraphrased 1 Peter 5:7: "Gloria, cast your cares on the Lord because he cares for you." Then she told me to text her a list of things she could pick up at the store for me on her way over for a visit later in the week. The truth of the gospel is universally applicable and immensely practical.

THE DEATH OF MATERNAL ANXIETY

The gospel is true whether or not we feel like it at the moment. A day is coming (quickly!) when we will all be raised together to life everlasting in the new heavens and the new earth. Until then, we get to live out our identities as new creations in Christ, encourage one another to put our maternal anxiety rocking chair out by the curb, and walk by faith together.

Newspaper headlines, worrying conversations in the doctor's office, urgent "buy this and save yourself" commercials, the chances of tragic disasters in our communities...the list goes on. All of these things have several things in common, but there is one thing they have in common that they will not tell you. *Every single uncertainty in this life* serves to point us to this profound certainty: because of Christ we can rejoice in hope of the glory of God (Romans 5:2).

The gospel is true whether or not
we feel like it at the moment.

This essay was originally published in issue 1 of Be Still Magazine®.

Motherhood Is Discipleship

KRISTYN PEREZ

I recently went on a walk with two seven-year-old "mommies."

I should probably clarify. I have twin seven-year-old girls, and the other day, we went for a walk, but this was no ordinary walk. My girls were dressed to the nines, with glittering purses and fashionable clothes. They held my old, fifteen-year-old iPods in their hands and placed wired headphones in their ears. They grabbed the stroller and gently placed their beloved stuffies inside so that they could walk around the neighborhood. As we strolled down the street, we attracted the smiles of more than one passerby.

When I asked them why they were acting like this, they responded, "Because we want to be a mommy just like you."

First of all, let me be clear about one thing: I am not fashionable. I don't go on walks with glittering purses or fashionable clothes. I don't walk around with my fifteen-year-old iPod or with wired headphones in my ears. They see a version of me that, while flattering, is inaccurate. But also, at that moment, I felt convicted. I was simultaneously flattered, humbled, and terrified. Man, these girls notice everything.

Motherhood is a beautiful calling. It is one of the greatest honors of my life to be able to love, pray for, teach, shelter, and protect our three little kids. But motherhood is also one of the most humbling parts of my life. As a mom, I fail quite often. Even on my best days, I can be short-tempered, arrogant, impatient, and rude. I don't reflect the loving qualities that Paul commends to us in 1 Corinthians 13 (patience, kindness, etc.).

Motherhood means having little humans who see you at your best and at your worst. Our kids notice the habits we have and the habits we say we have but don't. They notice what we love and what we say we love. They're watching, even when we think they're not.

Yet when I fail, when I'm short-tempered or rude—which to my shame can happen quite often—I have the opportunity to point to Jesus. I can point to the grace of God by admitting that I was wrong. I can seek their forgiveness. I can remind them that while mommy is a sinner, Jesus never, ever sinned. Jesus loves and pursues us perfectly. And even when I fail, I can point to the perfect forgiveness and grace of Christ, joyfully proclaiming that God's grace abounds. It is a beautiful and heavy responsibility to be raising little sinners, pointing them to Jesus through my victories and failures.

I was recently talking to a friend who was venting about her teenager's bad language. He kept using a select few words that were driving her crazy. But as the conversation went on, she confessed, "He probably gets it from me. I don't have the best language either." We laughed together and humbly remembered: motherhood is discipleship. We are teaching our kids what matters in life by the way we live and love. The question is, are we pointing our children to the Lord, or are we praising God with our lips while our daily lives remain unchanged by His mercy and grace?

Praise God, He can redeem even our worst moments. And thankfully, He allows every woman to be involved in the beautiful call of discipleship. Even if you don't have children in your home, you can still become a spiritual mother to younger gals in your local church. You can disciple, invest in, and pray for other women. Whether in the home or in the local church, let us not take the responsibility of motherhood lightly. It is a great joy and incredible privilege to shepherd little hearts to the Father.

Even when I fail, I can point to the
perfect forgiveness and grace of Christ.

This essay was originally published in May 2024 on The Daily Grace® Blog.

Walking with Jesus
in Motherhood

Breakfast with Jesus

JENNIE HEIDEMAN

Are you a morning person or a night owl? For years and years, I was a hard-core night owl. I could easily stay up until 2:00 or 3:00 a.m. Then, I started having kids. And, somehow, my babies did not inherit my night-owl tendencies. Instead, they took after my husband, who is an early bird. Soon, my 2:00 a.m. bedtime did not jive with my sons' 5:00 a.m. wake-up time.

Well, babies have a way of turning your whole life upside down and inside out and make you do things you never thought you would do. So, slowly but surely, my sweet morning birds turned me into a morning person. And, as they did so, God used my children to show me the beauty of mornings. For example, I began to notice the beauty in watching the last star give way to dawn. I even saw beauty in feeling the cold floors beneath my feet as I shuffled my way toward the coffee machine. But the most beautiful thing I discovered was the grace of having breakfast with Jesus.

This discovery happened about five years ago while I was in the thick of early motherhood. These were the years when it seemed like I would never again get a full night's sleep or be able to cook without a baby on my hip. During that time, I was doing a Bible study on the book of John. I was doing this study in the spring. So the days were getting a little longer, the Pacific Northwest tulips were peaking through the thawing soil, and I could feel my body and spirit awaking after a long, cold winter. This was the scene as I began to study John 21—in the afternoons, during nap time, mind you. In case you're unfamiliar, John 21 documents one of the interactions the disciples had with Jesus shortly after His resurrection from the grave.

In this account, Peter (the one who had denied Christ) and John were sitting in a boat early in the morning after a night of unsuccessful fishing. A man stood on the shore and shouted out to the disciples, "You don't have any fish, do you?" (John 21:4). When they replied that they didn't, He suggested that they throw their nets on the other side of the boat. Suddenly John realized who this man was. "It is the Lord!" he shouted. When Peter heard John's exclamation, he jumped into the water and swam to Jesus. Once on shore, Peter saw that Jesus had already started a fire and was cooking some fish to serve with bread. Jesus then invited John and Peter to "Come and have breakfast" (John 21:12), and the disciples ate with Jesus.

I love visualizing the picture of Jesus cooking a simple breakfast by the sea as the sun rose. I can almost hear the crackling fire, feel its warmth, and smell the sea when I read this account of Jesus. I also love Peter's reaction when he realized that the risen Jesus was waiting to greet him. Instead of remaining in the boat as John rowed it to shore, he jumped into the water and swam to Jesus. It was as if he couldn't wait another moment to get to Him.

As I studied this chapter all those years ago, something shifted in my heart. Though I was already beginning to warm up to the idea of my early mornings, I still didn't see the *full* beauty in them. However, after studying John 21, I realized that I have a loving friend who was waiting to have breakfast with me. In John 6:35, Jesus tells a crowd of people, "I am the bread of life...No one who comes to me will ever be hungry, and no one who believes in me will ever be thirsty again." God's Word is our daily bread, the only thing that can satiate us, and Jesus is ready to give His Word as our sustenance each day. I realized I wanted to be as excited as Peter was to meet Jesus in the early morning. So one morning, as my toddler and baby played on the floor next to me, I resisted the desire to turn on *Good Morning America* after making my cup of coffee. Instead, I opened my Bible and had breakfast with Jesus.

It has been five years since that first breakfast date with Jesus. My kids are much older now. I have had hundreds of nights where I got eight hours of sleep. And, I can't remember the last time I had to cook dinner with a baby on my hip. But one thing remains the same: every morning, as the last star gives way to the dawn, I sip my coffee and accept Jesus's invitation to read His Word—my daily bread and the only thing that can truly sustain me.

This is an invitation He gives to you, too. Every day, Jesus invites you to spend time with Him. You don't have to answer His call first thing in the morning (though I recommend giving it a try), and spending time with Him definitely doesn't need to be "social media worthy." But He is waiting to give you the sustenance you need, through His Word. Won't you join Him?

Jesus is ready to give His Word
as our sustenance each day.

This essay was originally published in December 2021 on The Daily Grace® Blog.

*Every day, Jesus invites you
to spend time with Him.*

Mothers Are Growing, Too

KATIE DAVIDSON

Each Mother's Day, my family gathers at my grandparents' farm. Pecan trees shade the driveway, bent over time by storms. Hydrangea bushes frame the front porch. Kids play hide-and-seek in the front yard while adults converse over glasses of sweet tea. Three generations of mothers are celebrated with hugs, flowers, cake, and kind words. Mothers, daughters, and daughters' daughters, all sharing one common title—"mom."

Once I was a kid at these events, but now I have joined the "mom club." And I laugh because as a child, I thought those in the "mom club" had life figured out. To me, they held endless amounts of wisdom. They kissed boo-boos, wiped tears, and mediated arguments. They were superheroes without capes, queens without a crown.

Now I laugh at my childhood naivety. Now I know the insider secret. Mothers are a work in progress, too. Moms grow just like pecan trees. Their wisdom is only as deep as the storms they have weathered. They bloom over time like hydrangeas. Motherhood is sanctifying.

Inherently, viewing motherhood as sanctifying (which means to become Christlike through the work of the Holy Spirit) implies that mothers are not perfect—in fact, far from perfect. We are growing as our children are growing. We are learning as our children learn.

This truth holds both freedom and responsibility.

FREEDOM IN SANCTIFICATION

In Christ, we are free from the yoke of perfectionism. Our identity no longer lies in upkeeping a perfectly manicured home or having perfectly behaved kids. Our identity no longer lies in our successes or failures. We can pause from trying to prove ourselves. We can come to Christ in our weariness and find rest just as we are (Matthew 11:28). We can find our identity in the only One who did achieve perfection.

Christ is our strength in motherhood. Ephesians 2:8–9 reminds us, "For you are saved by grace through faith, and this is not from yourselves; it is God's gift—not from works, so that no one can boast." Christ extends to us a love that we could not earn, forgiveness that we do not deserve. And it is out of this love that we can love and serve our families. We join Christ in His humility and humbly lay ourselves down to lift our babies, our husbands, and our communities up.

Christ's love transforms us through the power of the Holy Spirit. This is our sanctification. Day by day, conviction by conviction, prayer by prayer, our hearts are being softened and molded to look more like our Savior. This is a lifetime journey—a daily surrender. It means apologizing to our children when we raise our voices; washing the dishes again without recognition; praying and snuggling sick kids; and keeping our eyes focused on our true victory, the victory earned by Christ on the cross. In our lack of perfection, we see our desperate need for Jesus.

RESPONSIBILITY IN SANCTIFICATION

When we accept Christ as our Savior, we gain a purpose for our motherhood journey. The goal of motherhood is not to produce college graduates who are functional members of society. The goal of motherhood is to ensure that our children understand who the real Hero is—Jesus Christ. As Christians, the goal of motherhood is to make disciples.

But how do we make disciples while we are still sinners in need of daily grace? We humbly live out our love for Jesus right before our children's eyes so that they may grow to love Him alongside us. Deuteronomy 6:6–7 instructs us to keep God's words in our hearts, to "Talk about them when you sit in your house and when you walk along the road, when you lie down and when you get up." We are not given a mission in motherhood without a "how-to" manual. We come to Scripture for wisdom, for comfort, for rejuvenation, and for truth. God's Word is our greatest asset in motherhood, our greatest tool in fulfilling our responsibility to make disciples.

We do not need to wait for more knowledge or more faith to begin discipling our children. Christ is our strength in motherhood. He gives us what we need (2 Peter 1:3). He hears our prayers (1 John 5:14). He promises to be near (Psalm 119:151). We have a friend in Jesus (John 15:15).

Today, may the faithfulness of God bring us to worship Him. May our mouths be filled with gratitude and our hearts be filled with cheer. Because we have a promise in Scripture, a promise that we can count on. God will be sure to finish what He started (Philippians 1:6). Perhaps the greatest blessing we offer our kids is to allow them to see the real transformation of our hearts — real conviction, real repentance, real hope, and real joy. May this be our legacy that carries throughout the generations.

May God be glorified in all seasons of motherhood.

Christ is our strength in motherhood.

This essay was originally published in May 2023 on The Daily Grace® Blog.

Practical Discipleship
for the Busy Mom

TIFFANY DICKERSON

It was 9 p.m., the baby was finally down for the night—or at least until his next feeding—and all I could think about was going to bed myself. As I crawled under the covers, I realized I had not read my Bible yet again. Flash forward four years, it is 9:00 p.m., the toddler is in bed. All I can think about is going to bed myself, and then that all too familiar feeling of forgetting my Bible reading bubbles up again. That feeling is typically one of guilt, a feeling we moms are a little too familiar with if we are honest.

Being a mom is a wonderful gift from God. The ability to nurture, love, and point small hearts to Jesus is a privilege and simultaneously a weighty task. How do we point our kids to Christ when we are oftentimes so busy that we hardly have time to be in the Word ourselves? Days fly by filled with laundry, meal prepping, jobs, school, appointments, sports practices, and homework. In these busy seasons of life, how can moms intentionally grow in their walk with the Lord when they may only have five minutes? Below are some practical tips and reminders to help you as you navigate such a busy yet rewarding season. God knows every item on your to-do list, and He can be a part of each and every task.

1. *Get rid of the guilt!*

   Romans 8:1 says, "Therefore, there is now no condemnation for those in Christ Jesus." Jesus destroyed sin on the cross, which also destroyed your mom guilt and your feelings of being a bad Christian. Moms struggle with guilt over so many things, but Jesus has freed us from this so that we can move forward in victory. When you are tempted to beat yourself up over your parenting or your lack of Bible reading, don't waste time feeling guilty. Repent when needed and move forward to redeem that time for Jesus.

2. *Be intentional.*

This might seem obvious, but cultivating a thriving relationship with the Lord does take intentionality. But that intentionality does not have to be an hour-long quiet time at 4:00 a.m. before your household wakes up or at 12:00 a.m. when you finally drag yourself to bed. God knows these years are busy. Instead of spending one long period of time with the Lord, try spending several shorter periods with Him throughout the day.

3. *Post Scripture around your home.*

When my little guy was a baby, I had index cards with Scripture passages that I kept by my bed, the kitchen sink, and even in the car. Each time I was in those areas, I read the verses on those cards and tried to memorize them, pray them, or just meditate on the Lord's goodness. Having Scripture around your home will also point your reading-age kids to those passages. You can even get them involved as they help choose the verses and you learn them together. I might not have spent long hours in the Word on those days, but my heart was focused on the Lord as I went about my daily tasks.

4. *Be intentional about the books you read to your children.*

The books you read to your children can also impact you. We are blessed to live in an age when there are so many gospel-centered books for children that not only point them to Jesus but point parents to Him as well. Never underestimate the impact of the gospel in your own life as you read it to your children.

5. *Redeem the time in the car.*

Moms today can feel like a neverending Uber service but without the pay. As you spend all that time in the car, utilize it to sing worship songs, listen to a sermon or podcast, pray, or listen to a Bible reading app. All of these tools can point your heart to the Lord and even instill these habits in your watching and listening children.

6. *Find a gospel-centered community!*
Community is vital to staying faithful in our walk with the Lord. In these busy mom years, we can sometimes isolate ourselves from community using the "too busy" excuse. Whether you attend a Bible study at your church, host one in your home, or meet a friend for accountability and coffee, seek out purposeful relationships that point you to Jesus. These women can be a lifeline and support to encourage you in difficult seasons. Invite them into all of your emotional mess—and even the mess in your house. None of us have lives that are magazine ready. It is in the busy mess of life that Jesus can shine the brightest.

Over and over in the Gospels, Jesus simply tells people to "come." In this busy mom season, He just wants you to come, sweet sister. Bring the good, the hard, the ugly, and especially your tired heart to the feet of your Savior. He will carry you through and help you grow even when your time with Him may be shorter than you like. Jesus redeems our time when we intentionally seek Him. As your season changes and you have more time to be in the Word, by all means take advantage of it. Our intention to grow and spend time with the Lord should never stop. Your day is meant to be a living sacrifice before the Lord. Determine today to give every task to God, and you will grow right in front of your watching family. Remember that "He who calls you is faithful; he will do it" (1 Thessalonians 5:24).

This essay was originally published in June 2022 on The Daily Grace® Blog.

Determine today to give
every task to God, and you
will grow right in front
of your watching family.

When Spiritual Disciplines
Feel Burdensome

KRYSTAL DICKSON

I always look forward to January. It signals the closing of one chapter while opening another. It acts as a reset for my soul, looking back on the previous year with gratitude for what the Lord has done and looking ahead, excited for all the possibilities. With the start of a new year comes all the new things—a new planner, new resolutions, and a new journal to record the spiritual goals I've set for the coming months.

I start the year with good intentions. On January 1st, I spent the morning in prayer and reading the Word. Check. On January 3rd, the kids started back to school, but I did my Bible study in the car line. Check. Each chapter read in my Bible and each goal accomplished is represented by a check in my journal. But soon my checklist begins to look like an abstract work of art as the perfectly-filled boxes in January start to thin out in February, while March and April's boxes are sparse and haphazardly scribbled in. Seeing all those boxes left unchecked brings a sense of shame and failure. Surely this is not the abundant life that Jesus talked about!

Maybe you can relate to these "checklist woes" as you pursue the Lord through the spiritual disciplines—things like Bible reading, prayer, fasting, evangelism, and fellowship with other believers. Or maybe you can't relate because your time with the Lord feels more like a "Choose Your Own Adventure," deciding what to do in the moment. *Should I read a psalm? Maybe I should pray. What if I decide to fast this morning and let that count as my quiet time? That would be more convenient with my schedule since I won't have time to eat anyway.*

I have experienced both of these extremes in my walk with the Lord—falling short of unrealistic expectations and having no expectations at all. It's easy to lose sight of why we practice these disciplines in the first place. So what do we do when spiritual disciplines feel like a burden rather than a delight? Let's keep two things in mind as we pursue greater intimacy with the Lord through the practice of spiritual disciplines this year.

REMEMBER ITS PURPOSE.

If you have children in your life, you've probably spoken these exact words: "It's like you grew overnight!" Wouldn't it be nice if we could say that about our spiritual growth? Unfortunately, it doesn't work that way. We don't passively grow in holiness. Spiritual disciplines are just that—disciplines to be practiced through intentionality with consistency. When we neglect to be intentional in our time with the Lord, we tend to yield to our own preferences rather than the conviction of the Holy Spirit. These means of grace allow us to draw closer to Jesus as we set aside our own desires in order to pursue our relationship with Him.

Pursuing God through the ongoing practice of spiritual disciplines frees us from trying to operate in our own strength. Studying the Bible will instruct our hearts to see the beauty of the gospel. Praying gives us the opportunity to turn from our sin and walk in freedom. Fasting reminds us of our dependence and our need for God. The goal of practicing spiritual disciplines is not legalism, carefully keeping to a list of dos and don'ts. It is to produce a wholehearted devotion that comes from abiding in Christ.

REMEMBER HIS PROMISES.

God's disposition toward you is not one of disappointment, frustration, or impatience. He is a loving Father who delights in giving you good gifts (Matthew 7:11, James 1:17). If we seek Him, we will lack no good thing (Psalm 34:10). He does not withhold from His children (Psalm 84:11). On your best day, God sets His love on you. On your worst day, God sets His love on you. God's affection for you doesn't grow or diminish based on your performance. Your approval is found in what Christ alone accomplished on the cross.

Spiritual disciplines should produce joy as we abide in Christ. We can easily turn these habits into a performance *for* God instead of a way of deepening our relationship *with* God. God cares more about our hearts than our ability to read the Bible in a year. When pursuing God feels burdensome, don't lose heart. Fight for joy. Rest in what Christ has accomplished on your behalf. Reflecting on why we engage in spiritual disciplines will guard our hearts against unhealthy habits, while remembering God's promises to us will reorient our hearts to worship Him above all else.

On your best day, God sets His love on you.
On your worst day, God sets His love on you.

This essay was originally published in July 2022 on The Daily Grace® Blog.

Gently He Leads

SHELBY TURNER

I'm a young mom with a house full of little ones. There are smudgy fingerprints on my walls and windows, tiny socks littering the hallways, and stacks of sticky dishes in the sink. My sleep is interrupted and cut short almost every night. Tears and tantrums abound. For every ounce of love I feel toward my children, I feel an equal amount of weariness. Truly, in our home, the days are long, and...the days are long.

But, weariness is not unique to me or my season. I've found that most of us are tired for one reason or another. Your reason may not be the same as mine. You may be wading through deep emotional strain or physical pain. You may be working around the clock at a high-stress job. Or maybe sleep evades you because the world weighs heavy on your mind when your head hits the pillow. Deep inner fatigue is an epidemic, no matter the source.

And we're all trying to figure out how to keep living our lives while horribly exhausted. Some of us add things to manage fatigue: strict schedules, healthy habits, self-help books. And some of us take a different approach by removing things from our life to make the load lighter: less time with friends, less busywork, fewer commitments. No matter the approach, we're all just trying to cope with the pace of life and find a rhythm that works for our body and soul. In times of weariness, it has been a tremendous comfort for me to remember that God is a tender shepherd who gently leads. And I wonder if you might need this reminder, too?

Throughout Scripture, God is referred to as a shepherd who guides, feeds, and protects His people. The shepherd analogy is probably a bit lost on those of us who live urban lives. Shepherds are deeply committed to the care and keeping of their flock. And this is quite a demanding job because sheep are not particularly smart animals. For instance, if sheep graze in a pasture until it is barren, they will not move themselves to a new pasture with fresh grass, even if it can be seen from where they currently stand. They will instead stay where they are and starve. Sheep need the care and guidance of a shepherd to live flourishing lives.

And shepherds know the survival of their sheep is entirely dependent on them. They keep a careful watch on the state of the pasture, discerning the precise moment a move to fresh fields is required. As they consider each possible new meadow and valley, they must factor in something very important: the pace their sheep can travel. There may be sick sheep, wounded sheep, stubborn sheep, or sheep nursing young lambs. These animals cannot travel at a grueling pace. If they do, the journey will kill them before they reach the lush new pasture. They must pick a pasture that has everything the sheep need and can be reached at the pace the sheep can travel. We see an example of this in Genesis 33:13–14 when Jacob and Esau were traveling to find a new home: "Jacob replied, 'My lord knows that the children are weak, and I have nursing flocks and herds. If they are driven hard for one day, the whole herd will die. Let my lord go ahead of his servant. I will continue on slowly, at a pace suited to the livestock and the children, until I come to my lord at Seir.'"

God is the Shepherd of all who believe in Jesus. They are His flock. He knows when we need to move and when we need to stay. He knows the spots where we try to push His perfect pace. He calculates our weariness and the way our aches and pains slow our steps. When God leads, He leads us gently, slowly, and surely to a place where we will flourish. Isaiah 40:11 describes this beautifully:

He protects his flock like a shepherd;
he gathers the lambs in his arms
and carries them in the fold of his garment.
He gently leads those that are nursing.

Notice that some lambs need not even walk. The Shepherd carries them. Folded safely in the hem of His garment, wrapped in His arms,

He will not leave behind a single one. Even the weakest of us are safe in His care. God is attentive to the unique needs of all who are in His flock. He individually cares for those who are faint, injured, or in a strenuous season.

What does this mean for you and me? It means God's pace is good, and we can trust where He is leading us.

To those who wish to rush ahead when God has said to wait, He is never slow. Trust His pace.

To those who are sure God is moving too quickly, He has planned every step with loving care and compassion. Trust His pace.

To those who feel crushed and unable to walk the road ahead, He will carry you. Trust His pace.

To us all, God is shepherding us well. Let's match our steps to God's rhythm, knowing He gently leads us in each and every season.

God is a tender shepherd who gently leads.

This essay was originally published in November 2021 on The Daily Grace® Blog.

Let's match our steps to God's rhythm,
knowing He gently leads us
in each and every season.

A Prayer for the Overwhelmed

KATIE DAVIDSON

Gracious Father,

I know you are the source from where true, lasting peace flows. I come to You weary and in desperate need of comfort. My hands are full. I am ragged with overwhelm. My to-do list is much too long, and my capacity feels much too little. I feel afraid of letting others down, not meeting my goals, and not living up to expectations. The pressure that I've put on myself feels like weight upon my shoulders.

How can I be a good mom? A good wife? A good daughter, sister, friend, and employee—all at the same time?

Will I collapse under this weight, Lord?

No, no, I will not, for You are my sure and steadfast anchor. You promise that Your yolk is easy and Your burden is light. In You, I have rest for my soul.

I realize these hands You've given me can only do so much.

Help me to see my limitations as opportunities to enter Your presence.

Help me to see my weakness as a conduit to Your strength.

Help me to view my failures in light of Your abundant grace.

You do not expect perfection from me; You expect my affection. You do not desire accomplishments or trophies or productivity; instead, You desire my heart.

Lord, I confess I have sought other means of rest apart from You. Teach me to come to You with my burdens more, and tune them out less. Television, vacations, and self-care will not quench my thirsty soul. More money and more achievements will not satisfy me. I admit that running after these things—these temporary pleasures—has distracted my attention away from You. Father, I am so sorry. I do not want to settle for fleeting relief. I need Your lasting peace.

I confess that worries about tomorrow can sometimes paralyze my ability to engage with today. Help me to trust in Your future provision. Lift my eyes away from what is to come and toward Your face.

I remember when You provided manna in the wilderness for the Israelites. You gave them just enough for the day. And that was plenty. I know you provided for them, and you will provide for me. Teach me about Your unchanging sovereignty and faithful care so that I may grow in trust.

Father, I surrender my pride to You. I realize that my desire to do it all finds roots in my unwillingness to admit that I cannot. As a gardener plucks weeds from the midst of his crop, pluck pride out of me.

I surrender my shame to You, God. I confess that my weaknesses have brought unnecessary guilt into my heart as I try to live up to expectations I may never reach. This shame has no place here. You defeated shame on the cross, Jesus. You claimed victory with Your resurrection. Fill me with the joy of the gospel so that I can walk in freedom from shame.

I surrender my titles to You, God—the titles that threaten to define my identity. These responsibilities are a blessing, but Lord, I want to be a good steward of what You have given me. Use these roles to sanctify me, to teach me, and to extend Your love to dark places. The truth is, I will fall short in these roles most days, but God, You never fall short. I pray that You would use—even my feeble attempts—to build Your Kingdom.

In the midst of overwhelm, take me back to the basics, Lord. Remind me of my salvation, of where You've brought me from. Weaken my knees so that I may fall to them in prayer. Turn my attention to Your Word. Allow me to trust in You for daily bread.

God, I come to You in need of peace. I am tired and weak. Use me in this humble stance. Help me to reorder my priorities and simplify my commitments. Teach me to say "no" in wisdom and "yes" in gladness. Give me grace for today as I make the next right move. God, I long for the day when strivings cease and Your peace consumes the world. But for now, help me rest in Your unfailing love. Father, You are enough for me. Amen.

This essay was originally published in January 2022 on The Daily Grace® Blog.

Help me to see my weakness
as a conduit to Your strength.

Endnotes

1   *Merriam-Webster.com*, "enough," https://www.merriam-webster.com/dictionary/enough.

2   Bible Hub, "shalom," *Strong's Concordance* (2022), https://biblehub.com/hebrew/7965.

3   Bible Hub, "eiréné," *Strong's Concordance* (2022), https://biblehub.com/greek/1515.htm.

4   Dr. and Mrs. Howard Taylor, *Hudson Taylor's Spiritual Secret* (Moody Press: 2009).

5   Dietrich Bonhoeffer, *Life Together: The Classic Exploration of Christian in Community* (HarperOne: 2009).

What to Study Next

We hope that you enjoyed reading *Beside Still Waters | Finding Rest in Christ in Every Season of Motherhood*! Our prayer is that with each essay and verse you've read in these pages, you have drawn closer to the Lord and discovered what it means to rest in Him—no matter what you may be facing in this season as a mom. It is truly a gift for us to be able to know and love God, and we encourage you to continue seeking Him through prayer and the study of His Word. Not sure what to read next as you navigate your season of motherhood? Here are some recommendations:

1. *Grace in Chaos | Biblical Hope for the Hard Days of Motherhood*

   Do you ever feel overwhelmed as a mom—struggling with anxiety, despair, or comparison? For many women, motherhood feels like simultaneously the greatest responsibility in the world and the most difficult one. Thankfully, we do not walk alone.

   Grace in Chaos is a five-week study that will remind you of the nearness of Jesus, strengthen you with a biblical and gospel-centered vision of motherhood, equip you with God's Word, and encourage you with the truth that God sees you and sustains you in every season of motherhood.

2. *Gospel-Centered Motherhood*

   Gospel-Centered Motherhood is a short but impactful book that covers a wide range of topics related to the beautiful calling of motherhood. The book examines discipleship in the home, guarding your marriage, mom guilt, discipline, perseverance, emotions, and more. Every topic includes related Scriptures to meditate on and questions to consider to prompt prayer. This book offers a powerful reminder that motherhood is a gift, and the ultimate aim is to glorify Christ in and through it.

3. *Thirty-One Days of Prayer for My Children*

One of the greatest gifts a parent or guardian can give their children is the gift of prayer. *Thirty-One Days of Prayer for My Children* is a book designed for you to return to over and over again as you lift up your children year after year. Whether your children are infants, toddlers, teenagers, or adults, this book will help you spend focused time in prayer each day for their salvation, friends, future or current spouses, wisdom, health, and faithfulness, to name a few.

Visit www.thedailygraceco.com for these resources and more!

Thank you for studying God's Word with us!

CONNECT WITH US
@thedailygraceco
@dailygracepodcast

CONTACT US
info@thedailygraceco.com

SHARE
#thedailygraceco

VISIT US ONLINE
www.thedailygraceco.com

MORE DAILY GRACE
Daily Grace® Podcast